M000314511

The Palace Keepers

Protecting the Purity of the Heart

Jacy Lee Pulford

The Palace Keepers

Table of Contents
Foreword
Chapters

Foreword

**"For where your treasure is, there will your
heart be also" (Matthew 6:21).**

Purity: one word and yet so powerful. I can
remember when the word came to my mind a
few years ago, and I immediately thought of
sexual abstinence. In simple terms, I thought of
purity as not having sex until marriage. That is
a necessity, but the Lord started showing me a
deeper meaning behind purity and that the
issues of sexual sin lie in a more emotional and
private place: our hearts.

Following Christ and being a Christ-like
example means allowing the Lord Jesus Christ
to dictate every aspect of our lives, especially
the struggle to be clean and pure. The Lord
cares deeply about our physical condition, but
just as important, He cares who we give our
hearts to. Why are many young people being
led from God's hands and into physical sin? I
have the answer according to what the Lord
has revealed to me: It starts with what is inside
the heart!

It almost seems too simple of a concept, as if we should already know this. However, guarding one's heart is not a popular topic on our teaching /learning agenda. Have you ever thought about your emotional health? Why or why not? Church, the media, our friends and family talk about being in shape physically. It is important to live a life with a clean body, right?

With *The Palace Keepers*, I want to inform every Christian man and woman that protecting yourself physically is only half the battle. If we allow our hearts to be unguarded, we allow other people to control our emotions, which can ultimately lead to physical impurity.

It is our job, all over the world, to stand. Stand for what is right, pure, and just in God's eyes. Stand up to those emotions that try to control our hearts and how we feel. Proclaim in the name of Jesus Christ that we will not fall to a "feel good" nation, but we will stand and fight to be a part of the "follow God" nation!"

I believe emotional purity is the most overlooked problem today, both in secular and Christian circles.

What Is a Palace Keeper?

A Palace Keeper is a guard of the heart, mind, influence, conscience and body according to the Lord's instructions. It's a job that requires us to have King Jesus as our filter, helping us fight in protecting what goes in and out and what stays and doesn't stay.

This job is not easy but it is very necessary. The scary part is we're not taking this job seriously, if we even know about it at all! Other people are being our Palace Keepers and are not taking care of our hearts the way God wants.

This urgent dilemma is what has led me to create awareness. Throughout this book, information is provided that can help you on your way to being the best Palace Keeper for your heart!

"I beseech you therefore, brethren, by the mercies of God, that ye present your bodies a living sacrifice, holy, acceptable unto God, which is your reasonable service. And be not conformed to this world: but be ye transformed by the renewing of your mind, that ye may prove what is that good, and acceptable, and perfect, will of God" (Romans 12:1-2)

I'm not sharing this topic because I'm an expert or perfect. Perfection can only come through the Lord and His cleansing power, when we are sanctified and eventually when we go Heaven with Him. Through my private devotions, trials, conversion and spiritual battles, God has shown me some life-changing lessons that hopefully will bless you too.

We must stop aiming for perfection and start striving for purity. We must let go of creating our own fleshy measurement system of trying to become perfect by our own hands and finally lay down our plans to follow God. Lifted palms and open heart.

We must say, *"Lord, you see me, you know me and so please forgive me. For trying to play the role of creator in my life. Only you can satisfy. Only you can create perfect change. Only you can make my heart pure. So here I am…here is every broken part of me…here is my raw state. Pour into me whatever it takes to not only heal me, but make me new. Create in me a clean heart and help me accept purity by your standards, and lay down my idolatry of perfectionism."*

My Testimony

"You have to go through a test to have a testimony" Unknown

Behind every book is a story that started the entire process. Many times that story happened in a much earlier time, long before the author even knew that the basis of the story would lead to future inspiration. Twelve years ago, I definitely wasn't thinking about emotional purity. In fact, I wasn't thinking about anything pure or godly at all.

I did not go to church, let alone own a Bible. I did not follow a Christian life, let alone have a relationship with God. I had experiences in a Catholic church and CCD (Catholic Christian Doctrine) but never felt any spiritual connection with them. I was given some knowledge about God but nothing that went deep enough. *Maybe*, I had thought, *church is just not for me. Maybe God doesn't even exist.*

I went through the motions of high school and life just like a regular teenager; an emotionally-driven, boy-crazed teenager. My desires and dreams were all over the place, and I gave into almost every emotion for all the wrong reasons. At the time, it just "felt right."

I remember obsessing over the latest boy band and sprawling my crushes' names into my journal. I'd write sappy love songs about guys who didn't even know me and poems about being found by Mr.Right.

By the end of my senior year, I was really wanting to have a boyfriend. I thought it was a missing piece that I needed in my life at that time. I had built up unrealistic fantasies and expectations. I had thought my life was empty without one.

Before I graduated, I thought I had met the right one. We got along great and became instant friends first. However, something that should have stayed an innocent friendship very quickly turned into a heavy, long-term romance.

We sped things up faster than a speeding train. In the middle of this new relationship, I cut off people who had once meant the most to me. I was so wrapped up emotionally in this guy that I had become dependent on him and he on me.

I wasn't the zealous go-getter I used to be and I noticed he wasn't as driven as before. We had fun and got along for the most part but we also brought out the worst in one another. My heart began to harden, and my emptiness seemed to grow bigger. I put up walls to hide behind because I didn't want to admit that I was falling out of love.

I created unrealistic expectations for him, to try to balance my desire for a more wholesome life. We would argue constantly, and before long, it felt like we were roommates rather than anything else. I couldn't understand why I wasn't satisfied in the relationship. I thought this was what I had wanted. It was supposed to last forever, wasn't it?

Being a creative person has always helped me cope with whatever storms showed up in my life. Art and writing were my escape growing up. I knew that even though my world was not the best, I could create something with my own hands, and it would put me at ease.

As I was going through this chapter of confusion, my father introduced me to his best friend, Wanda, and she wanted to hire me to produce six paintings. Each one was a custom representation of the Lord transforming a life, one step at a time. Eager to paint for someone else and being a twenty-one-year-old starving artist, I agreed to the project.

The first painting was a very calming scene of Jesus' birth. Mary, the young virgin mother, was holding baby Jesus in an airy meadow. At that point in time, I was taken aback by the level of creativity it had. I never had painted that well before! I was feeling somewhat different inside. By the time I started the second painting, I began to meditate on the idea of God again. I remembered some of what I had learned from church as a little girl and the morals that my mother had instilled in me.

Guilt ran through my veins and I knew God was trying to reach me through this project. Perfectly timed, the second painting I was creating was of a throne room. The throne was placed in the center of the room, and three peasants were on their knees, worshiping around it. It was this painting that really ministered to my heart.

Just as I began to have a strong urge to know more about God, weird things started to happen. I began to have evil dreams, and my mind filled with perverse and demonic-like terrors. I would awaken at night and couldn't move. I would hear fire in my ears and feel shortness of breath. I knew in my heart that something was attacking me, trying to keep me from knowing the truth about God. I didn't know who to talk to, so I would pray the only way I knew how. I would recite the many prayers I had learned in CCD, but none of them worked. Finally one of them did and I know now that the prayer I uttered is actually in the Scripture, the Lord's Prayer.

One evening, I confided to my cousin Billy about everything that was going on. Billy is the older brother I never had but who is always there for me. We have a special, deep connection. Billy gave me a valuable piece of advice. He said the next time I felt like I was being attacked, to call out to Jesus and ask Him for a sign. He confessed that he had tried this and it worked.

I wanted help and was so scared, I knew I had to try it. The next night I got my chance. I lay there, trying to fall asleep, when I felt heaviness upon my chest. I couldn't move, and I flipped open my eyelids to see only a faint light in the darkness. It was my boyfriend on the computer; the monitor was the only light in the room. I tried to talk and move but couldn't. I then heard fire in my ears. I had enough of this spiritual attack, so I called out to God in my thoughts. *Jesus, I need You!* I cried in desperation, inside my mind. *I need Your help, Jesus! If You are real, show me a sign.*

Instantly, the darkness faded into a vision. The black of the night turned into a blue sky with white, fluffy clouds...and there He was. The Lord Jesus Christ, hanging on a cross with a crown of thorns upon His head. There was no blood, no tears and no anguish. Only peace. Jesus was looking down, and then His eyes came up and met mine. He looked toward Heaven, and then just as quickly as it came, the vision vanished. I couldn't believe it was real. *A real vision!* The darkness of the room came back, but the heaviness on my chest lifted immediately. I could move again! I looked around the room stunned, the vision still alive in my mind. There was my boyfriend, unmoving, looking at his computer. He had no idea what had just happened to me!

Needless to say, I got my sign. Within a couple of weeks, I made arrangements to move out. It was hard to end that relationship because it was my first of many things and we were good friends. But I realized that I was just staying because I felt too guilty to be the one to leave. I will never forget the day I left. It was raining the most I'd ever seen and combined with the endless tears flowing down my face, it's a miracle I was able to drive.

Eventually, he spoke up and admitted that we were holding each other back and this decision was for the best. Deep in my heart, though, I knew what this decision was what Jesus wanted me to do. Wanda took me into her home and became a nurturing friend and second mother to me. I finished three paintings from the series at her home. I was able to live there until I could afford my own place. When I was on my own three or four months later, following the Lord and building a real relationship with Him, I finished the last painting of the series entitled "Revelation."

During that time, I started dating my husband Jonathan. We spoke about life, morals, music, hobbies, and God. He shared with me that he grew up in a Pentecostal church and explained his Christian lifestyle, based on biblical principles. My heart ached because I knew I wanted that. Better yet, I needed it! I desired to go back to church, but I really didn't want to go just anywhere. I wanted to be purposeful. I wanted to know the truth about who God really is, so Jonathan took me to church one Sunday morning.

When I walked into the Apostolic Church of Enfield for the first time, it was as if the angels had descended and I was swallowed by their glorious worship. I had never experienced a presence of God so strongly, and tears began to roll down my flushed cheeks. I closed my eyes and felt arms around me. It was Jonathan's mother. She compassionately spoke to me that I was feeling God's Spirit. I turned to her and, from the depth of my soul, replied, *"This is what I want."*

In four short months, I received the beautiful gift of the Holy Ghost by evidence of speaking with other tongues and was fully cleansed by being water baptized in Jesus' name. With God's anointing and teaching, I finally had a revelation of who God really is: the one and only God and Savior, Jesus Christ!

16

Now here I am, years later, joyful for all that God has done. Jonathan and I will be celebrating 10 years of marriage this summer and we have two sweet boys. I am still growing and learning the things of the Lord, but God spoke to my heart back when I was first saved about this message.

I won't write that things will be easy once you surrender to Jesus or that you won't still go through trials. My first few years in the church were a huge adjustment period for me, and some of those sinful things from the past kept trying to creep in again. Yet I pressed toward the mark of the high calling and focused on Jesus. Eventually, what was an issue became dust, and what was once unclean became clean.

I am here to tell you that the time is *right now* to be your Palace Keeper. In those years I spent living with a boyfriend, doing things my way and not God's way, I could have protected my heart and body. I could have saved pieces of myself for my husband. *I had allowed someone else to be my Palace Keeper.* The condition of your heart is so important. Being your own Palace Keeper takes time, but be diligent. Then true purity will have its way.

This book will help focus your attention on Jesus and explain to you how to be a Palace Keeper. It is written so you can read it alone, with a friend, or in a group. The content will guide you and bring you deeper into emotionally purifying your heart. Everything happens for a reason and a purpose. I have always believed that. What I see now is that everything works for God's glory and for God's purpose. If you follow the cross and look to Jesus, He will be the Light unto your feet and will show you the right way to purity for your entire palace.

Let God create your love story. You will never regret it!

Chapter 1: Defining Purity

"The statutes of the LORD are right, rejoicing the heart: the commandment of the LORD is pure, enlightening the eyes" (Psalm 19:8).

Since the beginning, dark and light have been established in contrast with one another. Equality between the two is nonexistent because of their different attributes. Light, for example, is seen as bright whereas dark is seen as not-bright. The biggest example of this contrast can be seen in one day on earth. During the day we have light, but during the night we have dark.

Growing up, I was terrified of the dark. I know most kids go through this, but there was something about the dark that just made me uncomfortable and uneasy. Even as a teen, I had a small nightlight because I feared what would be in the dark if there was no light.

So what is purity? One source provides this interesting definition: **the condition or quality of being pure; freedom from anything that debases, contaminates, pollutes, etc.**

Purity is freedom from contamination and pollution. Purity is not bound in a sense by our physical bodies; purity is a way of life in our entire being. In spiritual terms, purity is freedom from sin. Comparing the different attributes of purity and sin, we will find a similar pattern to the comparison of light and dark. Purity is clean, holy, and righteous. Sin is unclean, unholy, and unrighteous.

If we take a moment to define what sin is based on these attributes, we will see that **sin is anything that violates or disregards purity**. It is purity's opposite. When sin is compared to the attributes of who God is, it is also His opposite. This tells us that we must be in opposition of sin in order to serve God and to remain pure.

To know the attributes of our Lord and Saviour Jesus Christ, we must turn to His living Word. As creation, we have a deep hunger to connect with our Creator. Some people believe this deep hunger is in no way associated with God. This causes uncertain and unhealthy lifestyles and choices because they simply are going against our natural calling. This calling is to have a relationship with our Creator and to know who He is.

"And I will give them an heart to know me, that I am the LORD: and they shall be my people, and I will be their God: for they shall return unto me with their whole heart" (Jeremiah 24:7).

We are made in His image and therefore must mirror His qualities. In order to accomplish our calling and to understand purity, let's look at some words that God has used to define Himself.

"So God created man in his own image, in the image of God created he him; male and female created he them" (Genesis 1:27).

Sin separates us from God, but purity brings us closer.

Here is a list of some attributes that define God:

- *Pure*
- *Holy*
- *Righteous*
- *Good*
- *Love*
-

There are so many examples and stories of how God expressed or exercised these attributes throughout the history that Scripture records for us. Many of us have experienced these attributes of God in our personal lives. Our King is great and has many more attributes that are not written on this list. These are merrily a few examples.

Pure: *"The statutes of the LORD are right, rejoicing the heart: the commandment of the LORD is pure, enlightening the eyes" (Psalm 19:8).*

Holy: *"There is none holy as the LORD: for there is none beside thee: neither is there any rock like our God" (I Samuel 2:2).*

Righteous: *"The LORD is righteous in all his ways, and holy in all his works" (Psalm 145:17).*

Good: *"Good and upright is the LORD: therefore will he teach sinners in the way" (Psalm 25:8).*

Love: *"He that loveth not knoweth not God; for God is love" (I John 4:8).*

An active process towards purity is required of those who follow God and His ways. If someone is not pursuing purity, the unholy combination contradicts the essence of God and the very image we've been created after. In a world where sin is glorified and purity is mocked, each generation of believers faces tougher trials and temptations. It is getting more difficult for us to keep the purity of our hearts but it is still possible.

When we let our guard down and do not have the proper safety measures in place to protect our purity and to preserve such a beautiful and God-like attribute, we allow sin to contaminate and to pollute us. Picture our hearts as a tall cup of fresh, clean water. Purity is the lid of the cup given to us by God.

If we are given protection to preserve the cleanliness of our hearts, why don't we use it? Is it laziness, lack of knowledge, misplaced priorities, or plain rebellion? Without the lid, it won't take long for the cup of clean water to become tainted. Dirt, bugs, food, and other things can be found floating around after a while. The minute we decide not to protect the cleanliness of our hearts and take the lid of purity off, we have allowed sin an open opportunity to defile and have its way. This leads to purity's other opposite: *impurity*.

When the process towards purity shifts and impurity continues, we can't be in line with God's ways. If He is pure and our hearts are contaminated without any plan to change, we can't possibly be mirroring His image.The Lord needs each of us to be honest and up front with the facts about our hearts. If we are not honest as the God we serve, the world will not see a difference in the heart. Then our efforts to spread His truth will be ineffective. We need to have that difference in our hearts! The world might think, *Well, why should I serve their God if they are doing the same thing I'm doing?*

Purity is meant to separate us from sin, not mirror it. The world doesn't need the lines to be blurred but distinct and bold. The world needs to see a difference between purity and sin so that those who come to God can experience a change. One form of holiness and purity is modesty. Being modestly dressed on the outside brings a clean image to the world, but God looks at the heart.

"I the LORD search the heart, I try the reins, even to give every man according to his ways, and according to the fruit of his doings" (Jeremiah 17:10).

I can remember fighting my mother tooth and nail about my clothing. She wanted me to be ladylike and classy, and I just wanted to be noticed. Deep down I yearned for the acceptance of my peers. What I didn't know was how big a message our image sends to those around us. Certain clothing results in a certain idea about that person. It may not even be in a judgmental way; we are just programmed to think such things.

What kind of message is your heart sending to those around you? Is your heart dressed in purity? Are you being emotionally modest? This isn't just something our Christian young ladies need to worry about. Young men in Christ are given the responsibility and the authority to lead the way. If their hearts are impure, anyone under their leadership, whether it be family or ministry, will be affected. This is not about gender roles.

Purity separates the ones who are obedient and the ones who are not. Purity divides those who are clean and those who are unclean. Purity binds Creator and creation. This topic requires us to look at ourselves in an honest and true light. We never want to do that! The truth is, though, that if Christianity is going to promote sexual abstinence and purity, we must also get to the root of that issue.

The root of sexual purity is purity of the heart!

We can protect our bodies with barbwire and still have our hearts open and busy like a hotel lobby. No matter how extreme our physical precautions are, if we are not being the guards of our hearts, our carelessness allows many impure emotions and eventually actions to take place. Worrying about the flesh first and our hearts second is a backward system. Our hearts weaken first, before our flesh breaks down. When we emotionally attach ourselves to others first, our flesh reacts to that attachment. Being a Palace Keeper is being the guard of your heart by protecting the many avenues that lead to and from it.

Chapter 2: Searching for Prince or Princess Charming

"And the Lord God said, It is not good that the man should be alone; I will make him an help meet for him" (Genesis 2:18)

About a month ago, a sweet friend tweeted a line similar to this:*"I can't believe everyone I know is getting married . . .except for me!"* My first instinct, to tell you the truth, was to tweet back something sarcastic. Instead though, I stopped and decided to send an encouraging word or two. Honestly, my heart was sad for my friend because she is still in her twenties. And I know she's not the only one worried.

The desire to marry is a huge motivator behind many relationships. And while wanting to be married is not a terrible thing in the least, it can cause some of us to have blinders on to real issues. Many young people, girls and guys, might be trying to mold a specific timeline for romance to blossom. This mentality of shortening the gap between dating and marriage is alarming.

When we put this kind of unrealistic expectation on our relationships, it's like we take God out of the plan entirely. It is possible that God will flourish a spark between two people in a short amount of time and will guide them to the altar for wedding bell bliss.

The reality may be, though, that God is not so much concerned about our relationships here. At least, that is not His first priority. His entire purpose and plan is for us to have a deep relationship with Him and to get to know who He is first.

Part of me can't help but think that the change of pace our society has exercised within the last decade is behind this. Everything now is moving faster, quicker, hotter, higher, and shorter; from extreme to extreme. Television shows are crammed into schedules for certain times of the day when the viewer ratings peak. Editors are cutting out so much that the show can fit into a small time-frame. We don't get to see the true nature of an episode because it's being fed to us quickly and then pushed aside for the next course. Subjects and themes are more grown-up than they used to be, and a lot of this happens in the editing room before the content reaches our eyes. Good, wholesome, purely moral themes have been dropped to the editing floor. Growing up, if any television show had one bad word or even one show of immodest skin, it wouldn't be scheduled until the wee hours of the night when the children were supposed to be sleeping, as a courtesy and respect to parents.

The fast pace of our society is causing us to react with fast-paced emotions. Instead of being courteous and respectful to God's design for our emotions to play out naturally, we are led to feel and then react. This is when we can confuse lust with love.

Isn't that what we really desire, to be loved? There's no harm in that. We are made to love. You know why? God is love. You and I are made in His image, and we are supposed to reflect love as well. We were also made to love Him.

That comes from having a personal, deep relationship. When you get to know someone, you first learn about their name. You learn their attributes and ways. You get to know their dislikes and wants. You learn their plans and what they want to happen in the future. That's how God designed it because that's how we must be with Him! We must know His identity, His character, His expectations, and His desires.

"Let all your things be done with charity" (I Corinthians 16:14).

Truth be told, I never wanted to date. I was not attracted to the idea at all, and this was before I was a Christian. There was just something personal about dating that made me hesitate and watch. Sure, I was a little insecure like any normal young girl, but this was something more. I think at an early age, God put something in my heart to warn me about the dangers of dating. He didn't say, *"Now, Jacy, dating is evil, and you can't do it."* It was nothing like that but more of a still, small voice just whispering, *"Be careful."*

I actually didn't date someone until the end of my senior year in high school, which wasn't the best timing. I was just about to move into college and start pursuing my dreams. I had already applied and been accepted to Bay State College in Boston, Massachusetts, as a fashion design major. I had waited for this moment my whole life! In a very short time after dating, I found that I was putting all my creative energy on the back burner. *How could I draw when I was in love!* I became so hyper focused on someone else to fulfill me instead of adding to me. Girls, we are known for this. Seriously think about it; we can go from admiration to lust, lust to love, love to matrimony in a minute! This needs to be reeled in and controlled or we might take action based off of unstable emotions.

Unfortunately at the time, I had no solid foundation in the Word. I didn't have a real relationship with God. Even though I was brought up with morals, which were enough to make me conscious of His existence, I lacked true knowledge of who He really was and what He expected of me. After one emotionally draining semester, I moved back home. I threw it away. I worked four years for this opportunity, and it took less than a year in this relationship to undo my plans. This wasn't his fault, though. He never forced me to move back. It was my choice, one that I made in the heat of my emotion. My heart was so focused on him, that I just didn't want be alone. My heart was not protected. So even though I had dreams, aspirations, and goals for my life, I traded it all for a piece of my heart that I will never get back. God tells us in Hebrews 13:5:

"Let your conversation be without covetousness; and be content with such things as ye have: for he hath said, I will never leave thee, nor forsake thee."

Be content with what you have and trust that He will never leave you. Don't trade in what you've been called to be for someone who may not be called for you! He was a great guy and I don't want to put him in a bad light. This story is about my journey and what God showed me about love. I know he truly loved me and wanted me happy. It was just not in God's will, and being together was actually hindering the work that the Lord was trying to do. We wanted different things and had different belief systems. It was hard for God to get to my heart when it was full with someone else.

Love is innocent and pure. There is a commitment behind the word. All too often, it is used too soon or at the wrong times. I was indeed "in love" during this time, but I knew he was not meant to be my husband. I had allowed my heart and body to be manipulated by emotions, and then I became empty from it all. More than that, I was hurting and grieving because I knew God was not pleased with the purity of my heart. I knew He had greater expectations but I didn't meet them. The good news? It's never to late to get right with God!

The search for our beloved prince or princess charming can be an emotional roller coaster. As Adam did in Genesis, we tend to "scope out" the candidates whom we feel would be our best match.

"And Adam gave names to all cattle, and to the fowl of the air, and to every beast of the field; but for Adam there was not found an help meet for him" (Genesis 2:20).

In order for something to be found, it would have to be lost first. Adam was not missing anything. He had everything he was supposed to have. God created him to take care of the garden and the animals. God created Adam to walk with Him so that Adam could gain a better knowledge about who God is and gain that understanding through a personal, one-on-one relationship. Yet Adam's heart was not content with just having God in the picture.He wanted more. So, he "scoped out" every living creature, in search for another relationship.

The young Christian mind-set has been programmed that marriage is necessary. However, this is just a small picture compared to the Lord's bigger system: His kingdom! In our search for a significant other, we can't forget about our real purpose. As Adam still took care of the animals and the garden, we must do the same. Though inside he searched for his princess charming, Adam never stopped doing the job God had given him. The truth is that marriage may not be in God's will for everyone. Before Adam was searching for an earthly relationship, God had created a relationship between Creator and creation. This is our first important calling: to have a relationship with the Lord and to know who He is! All other relationships are just secondary and possibly irrelevant.

We can't accomplish the other callings in our lives if this first calling has not yet been established. If we don't know who God is and we don't have a true relationship with Him, what are we here for? Lauren Barlow, a Christian singer, once said:

"God didn't create one Adam and five Eves and say 'Go ahead, date around and see which one you like the best.' He said, 'Adam, I know what you need and I'm going to create that for you.' "

What Adam didn't know while he was searching was that God had already decided He was going to provide a wife. In the chapter prior, we are given this revelatory verse of Scripture:

"So God created man in his own image, in the image of God created he him; male and female created he them" (Genesis 1:27).

In the bigger plan, Eve was already created! In the blueprints of the King's greatest project, Jesus had Adam and Eve already appointed for one another! If Christianity is to push anything on the new generations to come, it shouldn't be marriage. It should be a commitment to God. That relationship is the *only* one that really matters as we keep our eyes focused on the Lord with a vertical vision and not on each other in a horizontal vision. We must allow God to change us as individuals before we can come together as a team. I've always found this saying annoying:

"It's always in the last place you looked."

Really? I wonder why? Maybe because the last place you looked is where you actually found it! It's really funny how people have used this saying for everything. Then again, I can understand why. Sometimes we look long and hard for something and don't find it until the very last second, usually when we are not trying so hard. When you are searching and searching and searching for that special someone, your eyes may be too focused on all of the details, and you may miss God's will for you. In other words, you may be trying so hard to see what is east of you that you totally miss a predestined plan west of you.

The search for prince or princess charming would be easier if you'd allow our King Jesus Christ to find one for you. Maybe, in our human fear, we dread that God will not have the same taste as we do! Maybe we feel that this decision has too big of an impact in our hearts to leave it in the hands of an invisible being.

He is not just any invisible being. . . . He is the Lord Jesus Christ, our God and Savior! The One who created the earth and made the stars! The One who knows every hair on your head and conquered death! If He can make heaven and earth, I am pretty sure He has the capacity to find you a compatible mate. Trust Him!

This reminds me of a beautiful love story. No, it's not Cinderella and the prince or Beauty and the beast. These fairytale stories are great entertainment, but the reality is, they lie. Oh, come on, you know they do!

We can get caught up in the romantic themes that movies promote and totally miss the point. It's not about money, flowers, cards, or cars. It's not even about mushy love letters, perfumes, chocolates (gasp! I know), or fancy dinners. It's about the heart and if that person has it established in the Lord. When two people have their own personal walk with God and come together as one, imagine how much stronger that walk can be!

This story is about how God played out true love for Isaac and Rebekah. Abraham, Isaac's father, did not want his son to take a wife from the daughters of the Canaanites. The Canaanites were not God-fearing people, meaning they had no convictions and went about life the way they wanted, not the way God wanted. So Abraham sent his servant to find Isaac a wife from within Abraham's kindred.

"And Abraham said unto his eldest servant of his house, that ruled over all that he had, Put, I pray thee, thy hand under my thigh: and I will make thee swear by the LORD, the God of heaven, and the God of the earth, that thou shalt not take a wife unto my son of the daughters of the Canaanites, among whom I dwell: but thou shalt go unto my country, and to my kindred, and take a wife unto my son Isaac" (Genesis 24:2-4).

Abraham, because of His walk with God, knew the path the Lord had for Isaac. There is something to be learned here. Though sometimes it may be frustrating to be listening constantly to our authority figures, if we know that they have a close walk with God, nine out of ten times the intentions behind what they do are for our own good. Not many of us would be happy if our dad decided he would take it upon himself to find us a spouse! We'd get upset and probably accuse him of being too controlling or maybe even cop an attitude about how this decision is *ours*.

The fact is Isaac never did that. Scripture doesn't record Isaac blowing up at his father, storming away, or slamming the door to his bedroom. This was an arranged marriage, which is not something that is very popular nowadays. However, it's arranged in a different way than we see. On the surface, it looks as though Abraham was doing the arranging, but when we read more we come to realize that the Lord Himself was arranging. Abraham was being obedient to God's leading.

Abraham had a deep motivation for finding a good wife for his son. He knew that through Isaac, God would make a great nation. The Lord had verbalized to Abraham that his seed would lead to generations of people who would serve God.

"And I will establish my covenant between me and thee and thy seed after thee in their generations for an everlasting covenant, to be a God unto thee, and to thy seed after thee. And I will give unto thee, and to thy seed after thee, the land wherein thou art a stranger, all the land of Canaan, for an everlasting possession; and I will be their God" (Genesis 17:7-8).

We have to trust in the godly authority that the Lord appoints over us. We have to trust that their walk with God is so close that they know things we may not. The Lord has prepared them in wisdom and knowledge in order for us to be properly guided to make the right choices. Searching for a significant other goes beyond our desire for love. Who we end up with will have an effect on the plan that God has for us. Not having our authority behind our decision in who we marry will affect the job that God has given us to accomplish.

As the story continues, Abraham's servant obeyed and went on a journey, searching for a wife for Isaac. Genesis 24:10-14 records how the servant came upon a well outside of the city of Nahor and prayed to God to send him a woman. Not just any woman would do, only the one whom the Lord *Himself* had appointed!

"And the servant took ten camels of the camels of his master, and departed; for all the goods of his master were in his hand: and he arose, and went to Mesopotamia, unto the city of Nahor. And he made his camels to kneel down without the city by a well of water at the time of the evening, even the time that women go out to draw water.

And he said, O LORD God of my master Abraham, I pray thee, send me good speed this day, and shew kindness unto my master Abraham.

Behold, I stand *here* by the well of water; and the daughters of the men of the city come out to draw water: and let it come to pass, that the damsel to whom I shall say, Let down thy pitcher, I pray thee, that I may drink; and she shall say, Drink, and I will give thy camels drink also: let the same be she that thou hast appointed for thy servant Isaac; and thereby shall I know that thou hast shewed kindness unto my master."

Did you catch what the servant said? *"That thou hast appointed for thy servant Isaac.* Abraham's servant obviously had some knowledge that God was in control of this entire relationship! He didn't take it upon himself to find a mate for Isaac; he let the Lord bring him one! Before the servant was even done with his request, before he was even done with prayer, Rebekah showed up with a pitcher for water.

"And it came to pass, before he had done speaking, that, behold, Rebekah came out, who was born to Bethuel, son of Milcah, the wife of Nahor, Abraham's brother, with her pitcher upon her shoulder.

And the damsel was very fair to look upon, a virgin, neither had any man known her: and she went down to the well, and filled her pitcher, and came up" (Genesis 24:15-16).

God knows what we need before we vocalize it!

"Be not ye therefore like unto them: for your Father knoweth what things ye have need of, before ye ask him" (Matthew 6:8).

Let's think about something for a moment. In order for Rebekah to make it to the well at the same time as Abraham's servant, she must have started her trip long in advance before he reached the well. So before the servant even prayed to God, Rebekah was already on her way! Her steps were already ordered by the Lord for a divine and personal appointment. She was the *one* whom God had appointed; therefore, God had already prepared her for what was ahead.

It's not easy to see the path in front of you if you don't know where you are going. It takes trusting in the Lord and obeying His instruction to have peace that everything will work out the way it needs to.

The story is not done yet. The servant observed the situation before getting too excited. He didn't know which family Rebekah came from and had no real confirmation yet that she was in fact the one that *"thou hast appointed."* Remember, the servant was told by Abraham not to bring back one of the daughters of the Canaanites.

"And the servant ran to meet her, and said, Let me, I pray thee, drink a little water of thy pitcher.
And she said, Drink, my lord: and she hasted, and let down her pitcher upon her hand, and gave him drink. And when she had done giving him drink, she said, I will draw water for thy camels also, until they have done drinking.
And she hasted, and emptied her pitcher into the trough, and ran again unto the well to draw water, and drew for all his camels.
And the man wondering at her held his peace, to wit whether the LORD had made his journey prosperous or not" (Genesis 24:17-21).

If you believe that the Lord has sent you someone to marry, wait for confirmation! Your heart is sensitive and needs to be handled with care. Rushing into a relationship when your heart is not ready will have damaging effects. Just because your emotions are saying, "Yes," doesn't mean God is saying, "Yes."

"The heart is deceitful above all things, and desperately wicked: who can know it?" (Jeremiah 17:9).

When the servant asked for water, Rebekah showed kindness, respect, and obedience to a man she did not even know. She seemed good and wholesome. However, Isaac's bloodline was going to produce a great nation and great generations who would follow the Lord. A lot of authority would be carried through the family. Though God's plan would come to pass, the "wrong wife" could have changed Isaac's heart, which could have caused the Lord to choose someone else to use. No one is perfect, as we can read later in Genesis how Rebekah dealt with her sons, Jacob and Esau. She had imperfections and was a sinner, too, just like we are.

However, God knows how to "appoint," select, or designate the right mate, who will not hinder your ministry or the overall purpose God has for the chosen. There was a bigger picture in mind not only for Isaac or even Rebekah but for all of God's people and their future generations. So, you see, the servant had to be careful and make certain that Rebekah was in fact the one whom "thou hast appointed." God's kingdom depended on it!

You must be careful and make certain that the one you are with or have your eye on is the one whom God "has appointed." That is when the purity of the heart can help. When your heart is close to God and pure, it is more equipped to make the best decisions. A pure heart listens better in prayer. A pure heart understands authority and instruction. A pure heart leans more on God's way than the world's way. A pure heart truly knows God's perfect love and does not confuse it with temporary lust.

If you are confused about someone, it is better to wait for the sure signs. God is not the author of confusion, and He does everything in perfect order. Jumping before the water is ready can make a very dangerous splash.

"For God is not the author of confusion, but of peace, as in all churches of the saints" (I Corinthians 14:33).

Eventually, the servant received confirmation concerning Rebekah. *What would've happened if God appointed Rebekah for Isaac but Isaac started searching on his own? How would that affect God's kingdom?* **How would that have affected Isaac's heart?**

In the previous chapter, we discussed the differences between purity and sin and how there is a separation. The word *"**appointed**"* is defined as "*decided on beforehand or designated."* God had decided beforehand that Rebekah was to be Isaac's wife. If Isaac searched within his own designation, he could have become **disappointed**. This is, of course, the very opposite. *Disappointed* actually is defined as "*inadequately appointed.*" Isaac may have ended up with a Canaanite woman as a wife if he searched with his own resources, and that would've affected the purity of Isaac's heart. When we become disappointed in our search or even in a relationship, we have allowed ourselves to be swayed by our emotions and feelings and not by the appointment or selection of God.

Becoming someone's husband or wife is not the end-all role that God has for us. It is just the beginning! If you think your Christian walk will be complete with marriage, you need a reality check, my friend. Our walk with God is never done.

Marriage is just one step in the entire progress from death to life, sin to purity. Some of us may be destined to skip this step altogether! For others this step may be farther in the future. However God has it planned, we can rest assured that the purpose of marriage is designed to bring Him glory and honor. God is love, and marriage is a demonstration of that love. It is a privilege and not a right. If you are privileged to have this step in the plan that God has for you, wait until He appoints someone to share it with. Two appointed hearts are better than two disappointed souls.

"He hath made every thing beautiful in his time: also he hath set the world in their heart, so that no man can find out the work that God maketh from the beginning to the end" (Ecclesiastes 3:11).

God's timing is perfect. We never know what Jesus has in store for us. That is both exciting and scary. Protecting the purity of your heart is an important job in the middle of uncertainty. When we reach those forks in the roads or those rotaries, we can make sure that our heart is following after the right things and does not get sidetracked. With our hearts set on the Lord's path, we can only be *appointed* for greatness!

Chapter 3: Emotional Promiscuity and Purity

"Blessed are the pure in heart: for they shall see God" (Matthew 5:8).

When I used to hear the word "purity," I would give in to a way of thinking that most others follow. That is, when I heard "purity," I would think about abstinence and saving yourself physically for marriage. However, God used my own testimony to teach me something. He showed me, through the Scripture, that to be pure does not *only* mean in a physical sense. Purity must be applied to our entire person; our entire palace. When we have cleanliness applied to every part of who we are, our body has the ability or more of a chance to maintain its cleanliness as well.

"Wait on the LORD: be of good courage, and he shall strengthen thine heart" (Psalm 27:14).

"Let the peace of God rule in your hearts, to the which also ye are called in one body; and be ye thankful" (Colossians 3:15).

Emotional promiscuity is when a person does not protect his or her emotions correctly, causing several deep feelings to develop quickly within that one's relationships.

We emotionally attach ourselves to others, and they become competition for God's affection. Furthermore, we become so consumed emotionally in the situation that we lose sight of God's perfect love.

If we are emotional promiscuous, we become emotionally unclean. Our emotional purity is preserved when we reject being emotionally promiscuous and lean on God first.

The word "promiscuous" is used in the world as something of a sexual nature. I've always have heard this word being used when someone is speaking about the nature of a person's character. *"Oh, she is so promiscuous! She is with a different guy every day!"* When researched, the actual definition of the word gives a deeper understanding as to what it really means. According to an online dictionary, *promiscuous* refers to a lacking of standards of selection; indiscriminate, casual and random. There are dangers in being physically or sexually promiscuous. Not only is it against the beautiful sanctity of marriage, but it is allowing your soul to be dispersed among many partners, not as Adam felt when the Lord blessed him with Eve:

"And Adam said, This is now bone of my bones, and flesh of my flesh: she shall be called Woman, because she was taken out of Man. Therefore shall a man leave his father and his mother, and shall cleave unto his wife: and they shall be one flesh" **(Genesis 2:23-24).**

In the physical, promiscuity carries a risk of being exposed to sexually transmitted diseases and infections. Spiritually, this concept can be related to someone's heart that is emotionally promiscuous. We become casual and random in the selection of whom we give pieces of our heart to. We lack standards for ourselves and are indiscriminate. We allow our hearts to flutter too quickly, thus allowing our emotions to attach to many different partners at the same time or even just attaching to one particular person very quickly.

This opens us up to receiving unhealthy emotional damage. Some results are heartbreak, consistent loneliness, compromise of beliefs, fear of loss or being alone, obsessions, addictions, and idolatry (putting someone or something before God. I will discuss this more in a later chapter). Though there can be far more consequences, it's important to be aware of these. When we give pieces of our hearts away, we will never get them back. We can get caught up "in the moment," but our hearts can be lost forever. Not guarding our hearts and just giving pieces away can lead to giving away our bodies.

Relate it to an unguarded palace. Emotional promiscuity or impurity allows thieves inside our hearts to take whatever they desire and without discretion. The front gates become fully open, and all the valuables are exposed. Oftentimes this happens when we have unrealistic expectations in our relationships. We consciously or subconsciously create rules and guidelines for each other and then become discouraged when they are not met.

Emotional Purity is the clean state of our emotional health. When we are emotionally promiscuous, we become unclean in the purity of our heart. However, when we follow the Lord's instructions and allow our emotions to be dictated by Him, we become emotionally pure. The constant struggle between being emotionally promiscuous and being emotionally pure can happen every day. Being a Palace Keeper is keeping the commitment to purify the promiscuity by guarding your mind, your influences, your decisions, your heart and your body.

"Trust in the LORD with all thine heart; and lean not unto thine own understanding. In all ways acknowledge him, and he shall direct thy paths" (Proverbs 3:5-6).

Have you ever known or do you know someone now who is emotionally promiscuous? Are you? Here is an example from my own life. I can remember in high school having crushes on boys. Now, to have a crush is not a bad thing. We are human and are going to be attracted to the opposite sex.

For me, though, I wasn't just content with liking a boy. My mind would think about that person constantly, and the thoughts became a distraction from my daily responsibilities. What was worse, I started to develop very quick feelings for someone I hardly knew.

Within a week, I would go from liking him to loving him. I daydreamed about our wedding and the life we would have. In just seven days, my heart was open and vulnerable. Then, for whatever reason, that connection dissolved, and I would feel hurt and unloved even though we were not even dating! He barely even knew I had emotionally connected myself to him. It was okay, though, because in two weeks I would have another crush on someone else, and the process would begin all over again!

Can you relate to that? In somewhat of an obsessive way, I had emotionally attached myself to someone in a short time. That is emotional promiscuity. The worst part is that sometimes the habit never goes away, so even when you are in an actual relationship with someone, your heart can still be attaching itself to other people outside your relationship. This is how cheating and infidelity can happen. When we do not accept the job of being our Palace Keepers and preserving our emotional purity, we leave ourselves open and vulnerable to unhealthy emotional practices.

"Hereby we know that we are of the truth, and shall assure our hearts before him. For if our heart condemn us, God is greater than the heart, and knoweth all things" (I John 3:19-20).

Here is another example of emotional promiscuity. This is not a true story; however, the situation is similar to my personal example:

Jessica has been good friends with Ben for a short while. They are in the same youth group. What Ben doesn't know is that Jessica has been emotionally attaching herself to him for the past few weeks. Everything he does or says to her goes straight to her heart and fuels this unspoken obsession.

When Ben says hello to her at church, Jessica assumes he likes her. When Ben asks her to be his partner in a game during youth class, Jessica thinks he must not like anyone else. Ben has no idea the flame Jessica carries. In Ben's mind, Jessica is just a friend and they get along great. Saying hi to her is just like saying hi to his buddies. Plus, he wants to win that game in youth class, and she is awesome at it!

As it turns out, someone else was carrying a desire for Ben's attention, too. When Margaret ends up dating Ben, Jessica becomes depressed and withdrawn because her heart is broken.

Is that Ben's fault? No, of course not. Jessica had allowed her emotions to attach too quickly, creating her fantasy relationship; however, that was just a story within her own heart and not reality. Not to mention, she couldn't focus on Jesus, the main reason why she went to church in the first place.

Jessica starts to become less active in the youth group and starts hanging out more with "friends" outside the church. Every time she sees Margaret and Ben together, she grows in envy and hatred toward them. She begins to think it was Ben's fault. Week after week, Ben notices that Jessica is missing from the group more and more. He doesn't understand what is happening to his friend.

Before you know it, Jessica's emotions are attaching to other people, and soon she is compromising her beliefs to satisfy the emotional promiscuity. Ben never sees Jessica in church again.

On a separate sheet of paper, answer these questions honestly:

- *In what way was Jessica emotionally promiscuous? Why?*
- *What could Jessica have done to prevent this from happening?*
- *What steps could Jessica have taken to guard her heart?*
- *Why do you think Jessica did not protect herself sooner?*
- *If Jessica had done those necessary things to keep her heart pure, do you think she would be in church today?*

Think about this situation in your life. Remember, the roles of Ben and Jessica can easily be switched:

- *Can you see yourself as Jessica/Ben? How?*
- *What things in this example can you see being reflected in your own life?*
- *Do you have friends like Ben/Jessica with whom you have felt a connection?*

- *Have you asked God for His guidance and protection in those situations? Why or why not?*

There are many things that can happen when your heart is emotionally promiscuous. Some results are heartbreak, consistent loneliness, compromise, fear of loss, and idolatry. I know I am repeating myself here, but I want you to get this. Though there may be more consequences, it is important to realize the danger in giving your heart away and allowing others to control your emotions. Jessica had unknowingly allowed Ben to control her emotions. Even worse, Ben was not even aware that he had that much power in Jessica's heart. It was a simple friendship to him.

Having your emotions impure is an unsettling feeling. There is a constant longing for satisfaction and acceptance. God did not create our hearts to be dependent solely on each other. When we do not protect our hearts, we emotionally attach ourselves to other unstable beings and neglect attaching our emotions to Jesus first. God is our solid Rock and our sure foundation. When we attach our hearts to Jesus first, we become more stable.

Let's take Jesus' parable about the house built on the rock and the house built on sand. In Matthew 7:24-27, the Lord explained to the multitude the importance of having a solid foundation:

"Therefore whosoever heareth these sayings of mine, and doeth them, I will liken him unto a wise man, which built his house upon a rock: and the rain descended, and the floods came, and the winds blew, and beat upon that house; and it fell not: for it was founded upon a rock.
And every one that heareth these sayings of mine, and doeth them not, shall be likened unto a foolish man, which built his house upon the sand: and the rain descended, and the floods came, and the winds blew, and beat upon that house; and it fell: and great was the fall of it."

Sometimes we may feel that church relationships in our youth groups are so innocent that situations like Jessica's are not that important. We never know how emotionally connected someone can be to someone else or what is going on in his or her mind and heart toward the other.

During these innocent moments, we can prepare before things get out of hand. Jessica was too involved in her emotions to realize the dangers. It is my prayer that those in ministry roles as youth pastors and leaders will be more aware of the emotional purity of their youth and not just the physical purity. It is our responsibility to educate our young people and, hopefully, to help in preventing them from falling victim to promiscuous emotions and control.

It may or may not have made a difference if Jessica's youth pastor noticed her withdrawal and took her aside to chat about what was going on. We will never know now because Jessica left. Let us ask the Lord to reveal those dangers in our church groups and in our own lives.

" I will give them an heart to know me, that I am the Lord: and they shall be my people, and I will be their God: for they shall return unto me with their whole heart" (Jeremiah 24:7)

Scripture states that God has given us a heart to know Him. This heart we have been given has an initial purpose, one that gets blurred during our daily interactions with others. Emotional purity is not only for young people. Emotional purity is for all of God's people, meaning everyone on earth!

God loves everyone and wants the best for us, even for those who may not believe in His goodness. When something is pure, that means there is a possibility for impurity. In contrast, when something is impure, there is a possibility for purity. We must ask the Lord to show us our impure state, that we may recognize our impurity so that we may begin the process to turning to purity.

Having a clean heart dedicated to the Lord sets us apart from impurity and focuses on the purposes of God. The responsibility to retain our pure hearts is one that requires dedication, commitment, and diligence. A heart is a gift from God and needs to be taken care of with careful hands. Being Palace Keepers, we are equipped by the Lord with the knowledge and tools we need to keep our hearts pure. You will see within these next couple of chapters many things that will lead to this particular point.

A changed mind will change our influences, which in turn changes our decisions and ultimately changes our hearts. Only God can create a clean and pure heart, but as Palace Keepers, we have been instructed how to guard and to protect them by the King's instruction and guidance.

Chapter 4: Our Two Hearts

"Create in me a clean heart, O God; and renew a right spirit within me" (Psalm 51:10).

Here are some definitions of the heart, as defined by *Merriam-Webster's Online Dictionary*:
1: a hollow muscular organ of vertebrate animals that by its rhythmic contraction acts as a force pump maintaining the circulation of the blood
2: the emotional or moral as distinguished from the intellectual nature: as a generous disposition: compassion <a leader with heart
3: one's innermost character, feelings, or inclinations
4: the central or innermost part

Okay, so it may seem a bit silly for us to be analyzing the most important organ in the body. I mean, come on, we know all there is about the heart already, right? With the increasing knowledge behind technology, scientists and doctors are getting deeper into the mystery of the heart, a powerful, blood-pumping organ, and, probably the most complex, the heart's ability to store emotions and feelings.

For people who do not acknowledge our heavenly Father, the task to explain such a deep concept has led to much debate and confusion. Here are just a couple of facts about our heart, according to The Cleveland Clinic Miller Family Heart & Vascular Institute.

Your system of blood vessels (arteries, veins, and capillaries) is over 60,000 miles long. That is long enough to go around the world more than twice! The heart beats about 100,000 times each day. When attempting to locate their heart, most people place their hand on their left chest. Actually, your heart is located in the center of your chest between your lungs. The bottom of the heart is tipped to the left so you feel more of your heart on your left side.

Wait, your heart is located in the center of your body? Pretty symbolic, don't you agree? I came across a Web site that gave me some interesting facts about the heart as well, but there was one that stood out to me. They stated that at one time it was thought that the heart controlled a person's emotions.

When I read that, I wanted to know how a heart, made up of physical cells, can be responsible for something so invisible and personal as our emotions. Why would God create this sort of system?

I was pondering this question as I drove to work one day. I asked the Lord how our emotions could be stored in a physical organ. Instantly, He gave me a revelation. There are two sides to every heart, *a physical side and a spiritual side.*

"A new heart also will I give you, and a new spirit will I put within you: and I will take away the stony heart out of your flesh, and I will give you an heart of flesh. And I will put my spirit within you, and cause you to walk in my statutes, and ye shall keep my judgments, and do them" (Ezekiel 36:26-27).

The physical heart is the heart that scientists and doctors know about. They can see it and figure out how it works by experimenting on it. They can touch it with their hands, physically dissect it, and test it. They can analyze it closely and come to their conclusions about what kind of texture, color, and size a heart is supposed to have.

I think back to science class in middle school when the teacher said that I would be dissecting a frog that day. I said, *"What?"* We had to work in groups, and the teacher handed out a worksheet with the different tasks our group had to accomplish in our study. I remembered lifting the lid and looking into the box right at the frog's face. *Gross!* I thought. I wasn't a really squeamish kid. Blood never scared me. I would hike in the dirty woods with only socks on my feet. I never screamed when my cousin's pet python gulped up a half-dozen white mice, and I didn't even mind picking up dog poop! But dissecting a frog? Maybe it was the unusual smell, which was somewhere between the smell of burnt plastic and rotten fruit, that seemed to cling to my throat and shake my nerves. *"Ugh"*, I grumbled. *"You have got to be kidding me!"*

Of course, it wasn't enough to stare at the frog from the outside. The teacher wanted us to see hands-on the different organs inside. One cannot see what is inside just from looking on the outside. Fortunately for me, I was handed the tiny scissors to do the honors. One of the main tasks was looking at the frog's heart. We had to make note of where it was located and what it looked like. We had to open it up and see inside. It was physically in front of our eyes and accessible to our hands. To this day, I will never forget the smell that lingered in that classroom! You get the picture. Are you hungry yet?

The spiritual heart is the side only God can see. Try to relate it to our own physical bodies. We have a physical body, yet an invisible, living soul dwells inside. We cannot see our souls, but we know they are there and that they are from the Lord. That works the same with our spiritual heart. Only God knows the facts about that side and how it works. Only God can hold it and see it and touch it. He knows what it really looks like inside. He is the only Physician who can analyze it and fix it. Our only way to be diligent in keeping it healthy is to read His instructions, which are in the Bible. Jesus gives us the facts we need to maintain a clean and healthy heart.

If we are told by doctors and scientists that our physical heart needs to be in good shape for a better life, our spiritual heart needs to be taken care of as well.

If we know that eating a whole bag of Fritos isn't good for our cholesterol and can increase our chances of a blocked artery in our physical hearts, why do we think that we can just ignore what we feed our spiritual heart?

When God established our physical heart, He also put in place a spiritual part meant for Him. This part also stores all our emotional data gathered from our brain that the physical heart cannot see. However, when some emotions are poured into the spiritual heart, the physical heart can suffer from its intense effects on our human bodies.

Let's use anger as an example. When I get angry, my physical heart starts pumping faster. I start to feel an adrenaline rush throughout my body. I know some people get sweaty palms or pulsating veins. Our bodies are reacting to that emotion because the signals in the brain and our hearts are at the center. Even if the anger is stored in my spiritual heart, my physical heart can still pick up that emotion, and it ultimately prepares my body to react within the context of that emotion.

Let's use love this time. When you feel loved or love someone, that emotion dwells in the spiritual side. But your physical side prepares your body for that emotion. Butterfly bellies and, again, sweaty palms may follow. Your heart does beat faster as well, especially if the source of that love is standing right next to you (Oh my!). You may even experience shortness of breath and shaky knees. Again, it's your physical side that prepares for what is going on in your spiritual or emotional side.

This connection between the two is supposed to be harmonized to glorify God and to connect back to Him. When we allow God to dictate what emotions go into our spiritual heart, then our physical heart will automatically prepare ourselves for what God wants. It will prepare our physical bodies to be spiritually conscious and to react to those emotions more carefully.

When we find ourselves in compromising situations, having a heart that is emotionally devoted to God will prove to be the best resource for making the right decisions. But if our heart is unhealthy and not stable, it is weak in defending itself, and the physical part of us will be weak as well. Having a weak spiritual heart could mean that you have a weak God-consciousness. In other words, you are closer to the flesh than the spirit.

In the book of Matthew, Jesus came to a place called Gethsemane with the disciples. He told them to wait and took three disciples to watch Him pray. Though Jesus is the Omnipresent God, as a man He was still subject to His fleshy body and prayed as an example to the disciples. Jesus wanted them to witness how they should pray. However, when Jesus was done praying, He found the disciples sleeping! They were not watching at all! The Lord was so disappointed:

"And he cometh unto the disciples, and findeth them asleep, and saith unto Peter, What, could ye not watch with me one hour? Watch and pray, that ye enter not into temptation: the spirit indeed is willing, but the flesh is weak" (Matthew 26:40-41).

Really? One hour? This is the Lord Jesus Christ, the almighty God in the flesh, and they couldn't even watch Him pray for an hour like He wanted them to? Hold it. Let's ponder what we do in our daily walk with God. Do we give Him our full attention for an undivided hour? Do we have devotion and prayer every day with Him? Or do we get distracted and let our spiritual life take a nap?

"Watch and pray, that ye enter not into temptation." Be aware and alert. Be God-conscious by giving God time to speak to your heart in prayer and through His living Word. "But why?" we ask. What is the point of praying and following Christ's example? ***"The flesh is weak."*** When God became a man, He took on the form of a servant, a humble carpenter born in a manger. Jesus could have manifested Himself as an actual king, but He didn't. He could have been a rich tax collector, but He wasn't. Jesus' walk on this earth was not about what He could gain but it was about what He could provide. Jesus gave life through His death! His motivation behind all He did and does is His everlasting love for us.

When we "watch and pray," we give our Father and Saviour the honor and glory He deserves. By His flesh becoming the ultimate sacrifice for our "weak flesh," we have a chance to spend eternity with Him. Our physical hearts may be naturally weak. Through the duration of a lifetime, the steady thump will start to slow. Our walking pace snails to a stroll, and our breath becomes steadier. Our bodies naturally prepare to return to the earth as the dust that started it all.

Yet that is only the physical side. The more we invest our spiritual hearts into God and follow the Great Physician's prescription, the stronger our spirit becomes! Our physical hearts may lose a couple of beats or be completely off tune, but our spiritual hearts will forever sing! Sure, our physical hearts will start to weaken under the natural order of humanity, but our spiritual hearts will be strong by His grace and mercy!

As a Palace Keeper, in order to protect your spiritual heart, you need to stay awake. How would a king feel if his guards all of a sudden closed their eyes and drifted off to Never-never Land? Watch and pray, Palace Keeper. You do not want to miss what the Lord has for you beyond those pearly white gates!

Chapter 5: Palace Fit for a King

"For the palace is not for man, but for the LORD God" (I Chronicles 29:1).

When I think of a palace, I automatically envision an elaborate community of royalty. I can picture a grand residence, overflowing with the finest linens, polished marble floors, and exquisite gold staircases. In my mind, I always see the best of the best. I picture expensive decorations, one-of-a-kind finishes, and custom-made furniture. There are delicately placed, plush, white sofas! Hand-carved wooden accent tables from other countries! Soft, beautiful Persian rugs that go for miles! An Olympic-sized swimming pool filled to the top with ice cream, with a silver spoon slide! Okay, so maybe that last illustration was just for me.

The image we visualize when we think of a palace is something more appealing to the eye than your average home. What's even more glamorous, though, is seeing how beautiful the outside and the inside are. Before we can even get to the pulse of an actual palace, we must take certain avenues in order to get to the center.

What would you think if you saw a gorgeous stone palace with run-down, old, tattered furniture inside? We probably wouldn't think too highly of the person who does the upkeep. We would probably exclaim, "Oh my goodness, how can such a beautiful building be filled with so much junk?" We may even think that whoever owns the place doesn't even care about it.

"I beseech you therefore, brethren, by the mercies of God, that ye present your bodies a living sacrifice, holy, acceptable unto God, which is your reasonable service" (Romans 12:1).

As you walk in your daily life, you are a palace unto the Lord. Your body is holy ground, your mind is the gate, your influences are the courtyard, your conscience is the foyer, and your heart is His throne room. Different routes lead to the center of your heart. As a Palace Keeper, you are in charge of guarding every opening and presenting your palace in a pure way that is pleasing to the King of kings. The exterior can be beautiful, but what is important to God is how you dress your interior. What is the condition of your heart? Clean, pure, and gorgeous, or impure, dirty, and tattered? Have you been careful who enters your palace, or have you let your guard down?

Palaces are known for and even expected to have many things of high value and great quality within their walls. For example, million-dollar paintings from fine artists who are no longer with us may be hanging over the fireplace. We may have seen while touring a mansion or a castle these sorts of things. I know I have walked around some local mansions in Connecticut, wishing that one day I could inherit some of those wonderful treasures inside. The interior is cleaned to perfection, and everything has its place. That is exactly how God looks at our hearts. The same way I have marveled at the great interiors of the high elite, God wants to dwell in our hearts and admire its cleanliness.

Our hearts are made for royalty. As daughters and sons of the almighty King Jesus, He would love our hearts to be poised with dignity, filled with high value and great quality things, having all good treasures in their rightful places. However, just having it all prepared with the "best of the best" is not enough. Preparation is important, but so is the upkeep. Once everything is polished and decorated, who is going to take care of it all? After a while, those pretty little tables will get dusty. The floors lose their shine, and the windows fill with water spots. So the king appoints staff to help care for the palace. The most important position the King needs filled immediately is a Palace Keeper!

Can you imagine a house so divine without someone to watch who is coming in and out at all times? Or not having anyone to delegate responsibilities, that the king's orders are accomplished properly? No, not having a palace keeper could be devastating.

Palace keepers are responsible for guarding the entire palace and bringing a sense of security. Without one, there would be no one to stop thieves from gathering all the pricey goods and walking right out the front doors! The king would not be safe, and his precious treasures would be gone.

That is why the King needs you! He needs a Palace Keeper for your heart, someone to protect the treasures that mean the most to Him, who will watch over the entire palace and keep eyes watchful in all directions. There is no telling what can happen if you don't do your job! The Lord Jesus Christ is the King of kings, the highest dedication in royalty. He is a patient and humble King. He is the One and only King and should be treated with the utmost respect.

We must make a decision to place Jesus where He belongs, sitting in the throne room of our hearts. *After all, what is a king without a throne?* Jesus has given us the power of choice to follow Him. As our Father, He wants us to follow Him with understanding and a willing heart. A forced action can result in an empty commitment. As a parent, when a child willingly commits to completing a job because he loves you and wants to please you, that reward is much greater.

This is how we must approach the Lord:
1.) Father, what will You like me to do?
2.) How would You like it done?
3.) If I feel unwilling, can You reveal to me why?

Jesus knows and sees all things. There is a path for our life, but God gives us the choice to walk it. It is up to us to accept the job as the Palace Keeper! The end reward is much greater with a willing heart who wants to step up than with one who just went through the motions and is only staying level.

"I will behave myself wisely in a perfect way. O when wilt thou come unto me? I will walk within my house with a perfect heart" (Psalm 101:2).

In a previous chapter, we talked about how God selected Rebekah for Isaac. King Jesus has a way of preparing us for what is to come. The Lord has already designated that our palaces be a place where He can dwell. His kingdom must first be established within us before we can establish it in the world.

"Neither shall they say, Lo here! or, lo there! for, behold, the kingdom of God is within you" (Luke 17:21).
"That ye would walk worthy of God, who hath called you unto his kingdom and glory" (I Thessalonians 2:12).

Chapter 6: Your Self-worth

Yup, you've been there. Staring in the mirror, thinking, *My God, are you serious? Why did You make me look like this?* If you have never had this encounter, you are either headless or a ghost, or perhaps both. For me, I didn't like my smile, my body, or my unique quirks. Basically everything! I thought I was weird and awkward. Most of the time, I still do.

God has created you in a special way. He formed everything about you: your looks, personality, talents, and essence. It's easy to think that we have to look to other people in order to define who we are. What is even more amazing is that God has called us to be someone and yet we often feel very inadequate because of how we perceive our self-worth.

According to familyfirstaid.org, a questionnaire was given to ninety thousand students in grades seven through twelve. It showed that the majority agreed that self-esteem helps teens deal with emotional stress. Some of those stresses are appearance, fellow peers, living up to their parents' expectations, and/or unrealistic expectations. Mind you, these are just some examples and from a secular resource.

Another website, selfgrowth.com, provides a deeper look into the actual definition of self-esteem and what it means.

They state that self-esteem is a condition or a state of being. The National Association of Self Esteem (NASE) defines self-esteem as **"the _experience_ of being capable of meeting life's challenges and being _worthy of happiness_."**

That makes sense. When we look at ourselves, we often wonder if we are worthy—worthy of happiness, love, joy, peace, understanding, and lots of other things. We experience so much that shapes our idea of who we are and how people perceive us.

As a Christian, I know that the word "self" needs to be handled with care. We are not called "Self-tian" though we do act like that. To be a Christian is to be "Christ-like." We have this life for Jesus, to glorify Him. If we are so busy looking at our "self," our focus gets taken off Christ. Instead of self-esteem, let's use _self-worth_. That's a different tone than self-esteem, _but what is self-worth?_

Self-worth is the value of what you perceive you are worth as a person. To be "worth" something, we have to have a price. If we feel a high level of self-worth, we seem to have higher standards and expect a higher level of respect. If we have low self-worth, we feel like we have no value and no respect.

I used to think that my self-worth depended on the people around me, that if I measured up to certain people who I thought had a higher level of self-worth, it would somehow, miraculously rub off on me.

What that did was just cause me to feel worse about myself as a person! I felt like a fake and a loser. I was trying to measure my value by comparing it to other humans.

The amazing thing is, we can look at the Scriptures, and Jesus lets us know exactly how much each of us are worth!

"Let this mind be in you, which was also in Christ Jesus: who, being in the form of God, thought it not robbery to be equal with God: but made himself of no reputation, and took upon him the form of a servant, and was made in the likeness of men: and being found in fashion as a man, he humbled himself, and became obedient unto death, even the death of the cross" (Philippians 2:5-8).

God reminds us that each of us has worth; true worth. *How do we know?* By looking at the price that Jesus paid for our opportunity of salvation! We can measure our true worth by what He has done for all of us: becoming the sacrifice for our sins so that we may have eternal life!

Jesus died for us on the cross at Calvary, shedding His own blood for His precious sons and daughters. Surely through that revelation we see how much we are worth. When we look at our self-worth, we usually compare ourselves to others, and that is how we determine what our value is.

This is awful to do because we are all humans and are all guilty of sin. *Why do we seek approval and measurement of worth from each other?* When we realize that the price for our salvation was paid by His blood because of how much He loves us, that's when we see our true worth in Jesus. He thought we were worth His own life!

"Hearken, my beloved brethren, Hath not God chosen the poor of this world rich in faith, and heirs of the kingdom which he hath promised to them that love him?" (James 2:5).

Through the love that Jesus has shown, through His selfless sacrifice for us, we grow to love our God. Your self-worth is not defined by what others say and do; it's defined by what Jesus said and did!

"I am the door: by me if any man enter in, he shall be saved, and shall go in and out, and find pasture. The thief cometh not, but for to steal, and to kill, and to destroy: I am come that they might have life, and that they might have it more abundantly. I am the good shepherd: the good shepherd giveth his life for the sheep" (John 10:9-11).

Wow! Jesus said not only that He is the door where we may enter in, but also that He is the Good Shepherd! As both God and Savior, Jesus showed us how much He loves us that day at Calvary.

In our daily lives, it's hard not to compare ourselves with each other. The way we measure our self-worth is when we look horizontally. Looking at each other, we cannot help but feel like there is a certain criteria we need to follow in order to be worthy of love and/or appreciated.

As we are looking around, we see Hollywood pushing its view on what is beautiful and what is worthy into homes across the world. When we are bombarded by these images and themes, how does that make us feel? Television rarely shows how much time, effort, and money go into creating all the popular looks and trends. Hollywood doesn't share all the behind-the-scene editing that magazines do before photos hit print.

Actually, every photo that graces magazine covers across America has been photoshopped and/or altered in some way. Photos of celebrities and models usually undergo intense editing before making it to our watchful eyes.

Back in the fall of 2009, famous American fashion designer Ralph Lauren became a target under fire after an ad featuring a horrifically altered model raised eyebrows and questions about how the fashion industry pushes "perfection." The ad showed a well-known model's head badly photoshopped onto a very thin body. Unfortunately, the model featured had been fired in the spring for not meeting Ralph Lauren's "standards."

Since the dawn of time, the idea of what a person's look or weight should be has made us question our God-given stature. All these aspects affect the emotions of our hearts and how we guard our palaces. When we don't feel adequate, we naturally tend to want to change ourselves to fit a popular mold. This leaves our heart wandering, trying to fit into places it's not meant to fit into.

Jesus made us all a certain way for a reason and a purpose. The author of Psalm 139:14 told God:

"I will praise thee; for I am fearfully and wonderfully made: marvellous are thy works; and that my soul knoweth right well."

I took the liberty of setting up my own online polls in which I encouraged my family and friends to vote on questions dealing with emotional purity. Here are the following questions I asked and the answers that were received:

Do you think emotional purity is an issue in today's generation?
Absolutely, 55.56%
Sort of, 33.33%
Don't Know, 0%
No, 11.11%

Who is the biggest influence (besides God) in your life?
Spouse/Boyfriend/Girlfriend, 60%
Parent/Sister/Brother/Aunt/Uncle, etc., 20%
Pastor/Pastor's Wife/Youth Leader, etc., 0%
Celebrity/Public Figure, 0%
Other, 20%
Have you heard the term "emotional purity"
before?
Yes, 100%
No, 0%
In what age group do you feel emotional purity can be an issue?
Young Child Stage (2-9 yrs old) 0%
In Between Stage (10-13 yrs old) 0%
Teenager Stage (14-18 yrs old) 100%
Young Adult Stage (19-25 yrs old) 0%
Other (26+) 0%

Pretty interesting, isn't it? Though most of the results I was not surprised with, some made me think. While preparing for this book, I told the summary of what I felt the Lord wanted me to write to people of different ages. I was in awe by how many people *over* the teenager stage spoke up and said they *needed* to read this book! What's more, those people are over the age of forty.

My intention for this book was to focus on our youth and their purity. However, the Lord showed me that purity knows no age and has led me to write deeper as this project went on. God made us in a wonderful way. He is an individual God, a Father who cares about His children and who they are because He made us all with pure love. He made you! Jesus cares about where you are emotionally and how you are feeling about yourself. He is there to listen and to help us, just like an earthly father would.

Emotional promiscuity can stem from giving someone else or others control over your self-worth. It may not be intentional, but it is very easy to be influenced by other people's opinions and to start believing them as facts.

How proud were you when you came home as a kid from school and presented your mother a clay pot from art class? To you, in your perspective, it was amazing! You were glowing. You felt a high level of self-worth because you accomplished something and you were giving it to someone you loved. Yes, it wasn't perfect, but you made it with blood, sweat, and tears. Well, as much as any third-grader can.

Now, your mother would never tell you up front that it wasn't nice. The clay pot wasn't good enough. *You could have tried harder, sculpted the pot smoother, chose better colors. It has faults, kid; are you blind?* Instead, your mother accepted the gift because it was already acceptable to you, the creator! And most importantly, you were the one she loved and cherished. Sure, she may not know what to do with it. It may sit on the coffee table and hold a remote control or sit on a desk for paper clips. Who knows! The bottom line is that your mother displayed it like she had paid a million dollars for it because you made it for her.

When the Lord creates you, He hands you a wonderfully made clay pot. Not perfect, still workable and maybe slightly cracked, but cherished and loved nonetheless. You may look into the mirror and see a lopsided pot, but God sees something worth more than a million dollars. He sees something that is worth the price of His own life! He created you with love; therefore, if you love God, accept what He has made.

Now, do not mistake me for suggesting that we need to accept our sinful nature or impurity. This is not the case. What I am trying to say is that God made you special, to be set apart. We are meant for more than this world has to offer! Stop bashing the way you look or your personality type. Those things were wonderfully made by the hand of God! *Why conform His creation to a world that doesn't really appreciate His work?*

"And be not conformed to this world: but be ye transformed by the renewing of your mind, that ye may prove what is that good, and acceptable, and perfect will of God" **(Romans 12:2).**

When you have the knowledge that the almighty God humbled Himself and became a man to give your soul an opportunity to be saved, you will "experience the worthiness of happiness!"

So, what does self-worth have to do with emotional promiscuity? Why is self-worth so important to keep your emotions pure?

These may seem like obvious questions, but think about them for a minute. When we don't feel good enough because we are comparing ourselves to one another or we want to feel better in certain areas of our life, particularly relationships, we knowingly or unknowingly quit guarding our palace and make compromises. We end up giving away pieces of our heart to people, and they start controlling our emotions. We then have no more pieces of our hearts left for that special someone whom God has appointed for us because we gave it all away. We are not perfect, but having a willing heart to change is the best place to start. It will open us up to God and give Him the green light in perfecting us.

Leaving our heart unguarded is like leaving the back door to the kitchen open when we have made homemade apple pie. It's sweet and enticing. The aroma of the delicious dessert floats gently out the open door and grabs the attention of whoever is passing by. Naturally, he or she follows the smell right inside our kitchen!

If we leave the door open, who is going to knock? Especially with homemade apple pie! You won't find me knocking; I'll just help myself, thank you! It is an invitation. Even if we didn't leave the door open on purpose, we left an open invitation to unfamiliar or unwanted guests.

**"In the house of the righteous is much
treasure: but in the revenues of the wicked
is trouble" (Proverbs 15:6).**

Think of the world as a bad neighborhood
and your heart as your home. Would you leave
your door open when crime is happening right
on your front steps? Of course not! Treat your
heart like you would your home. Better yet,
treat it like a palace!

**"I will behave myself wisely in a perfect
way. O when wilt thou come unto me? I will
walk within my house with a perfect heart"
(Psalm 101:2).**

Would we let unwanted or unfamiliar
strangers from the streets into our houses,
using our toothbrushes and sleeping in our
beds? Let us not accept unwanted or unfamiliar
tendencies into our hearts, using our emotions
and controlling our mind. Ask yourself these
questions:

*How do I feel about my self-worth when no
one else is around?*
*Do I feel overwhelmed and depressed when
I'm alone?*
*Am I only uplifted around other people like
friends?*

When I look in the mirror, am I happy with what I see?
Am I truly happy with God?
Do I try to seek approval from others around me?
When was the last time I complimented myself?

The truth is that no one knows, not even you, how much value your life really has, except for our King, Jesus Christ. No one can or will ever make you feel more beautiful than the hands that made you. God took the time and love to assign you special gifts and attributes. He is the only One who knows how you were constructed and what your true potential is.

Nothing anyone says about you on this earth can touch the magnitude of how God feels about you. Think about the best compliment you have ever received. Now think about this one: Jesus thought that you were so valuable, He paid the price for you with His life.

He is the One who knows your true value because you are His precious creation. You are His daughter. You are His son. And nothing we do or this world does can or will change that fact.

Chapter 7: Overcoming Inward Challenges

Every so often someone gets inspired by the different circumstances that they've experienced in life and feel they have a story to tell. I am no different and feel like that right now. The problem is that I have never written a book in my life, and it is a bit intimidating. Okay, really intimidating! Nevertheless, every time I turn around, it seems like God keeps pointing an arrow to my writing corner. When I was a little girl, I loved to write. Besides immersing myself in art as therapy for my awkward socialness and personal trials, writing took me into another world, where I could escape.

Growing up is tough for a girl. It doesn't matter what race you are or what religion you are, believe me when I say that it is hard! Really, it's tough growing up in general. There are daily distractions, daily interactions, and daily data that our minds voluntarily and involuntarily process all the time. For a person who is just learning life for the first time, trying to figure out what is good and what is bad for us can get complicated.

I never felt like a cool person. You know, the one who always has the huge group of friends to hang out with. The one who always knew what to say and what to do and did it the best. Or the one who could walk on water and had gold running through her veins. Yeah, I never felt like that person. For me, there were a number of things that I was unhappy with about myself that I felt others had going for them. Between fashion and friends, I was constantly comparing myself to everybody else.

My biggest issue? I really disliked my face. Pretty sad since that is not something you can just trade in, like an old car. Well, not without paying a huge price! It wasn't everything about it, but certain features I felt took away from the beauty that I wanted to portray. I think early in our childhood, we tend to create our own idols to look to because of what we feel we're lacking in ourselves. There's a difference between admiration and obsession.

When we have **admiration** for someone, we admire their character, personality, and other traits. We don't overdo our appreciation, but we find that person intriguing. There is something about them that we find refreshing. When we have an **obsession** for someone, we are *overly* admiring. Our thoughts and our hearts work overtime thinking and/or comparing ourselves to that person and appreciation for them goes to the extreme. We don't just find that person refreshing; it's like we can't even breathe without them!

We can admire or obsess over just about anyone or anything. Protecting your heart isn't just about dating relationships, but it's about all relationships and protecting us from all distractions. A friend, family member, church member, teacher, movie star, or famous celebrity can be an idol in our life. On the other hand, so can the Internet, work, or a sport.

The reason I bring this up is because we can feel so inadequate about ourselves that we turn to other people or things to try to compensate. For me, I had a hard time with my physical appearance, so I obsessed over Hollywood celebrities.

Here is a detailed definition of what an "**idol**" is:

1.) An image or other material object representing a deity to which religious worship is addressed.
2.) An image of a deity other than God.
3.) Any person or thing regarded with blind admiration, adoration, or devotion
4.   ) A figment of the mind; fantasy.

Now, it is great to have role models and to be involved in activities you love. I am not suggesting that you cannot look up to a positive, godly influence and appreciate what he/she represents or play a fun game of volleyball.

Caution takes place when we allow people and things to take first place in our lives, instead of Jesus. I personally never felt good enough, so I would look up to people who I thought were great. *That is simple logic, right?* God's Word, however, states that it is actually a sin against God to look up to anyone or anything else *more* than God himself. It is called "**idolatry**." It is when we look up to other people or things first and God second . . . or even third . . . or even fourth . . . or even . . . well, you get it.

In the Book of Exodus, Moses helped the people of Israel escape out of Egypt. In chapter 32, Moses took so long on the mountain speaking with the Lord that the people below became restless. They approached Moses' brother, Aaron, and expressed their discomfort with the situation.

Aaron gathered all the gold earrings from the people of Israel, melted them, and created a golden calf. He told the Israelites to accept the golden calf as their new god and even told them that the calf had brought them out of Egypt! The Lord sent Moses down to confront the idolatry and repented of the evil that He thought to do unto those who betrayed Him.

"But ye shall destroy their altars, break their images, and cut down their groves: for thou shalt worship no other god" (Exodus 34:13-14).

When you are a Palace Keeper, you must be aware of the different images that may try to lure you from your duties. Having a role model who is pleasing to God, such as a youth pastor or worship leader, is a great thing. Also, if you are involved in after-school programs or hobbies, those are good for our productivity. However, we must never replace God! He shall always be our first role model and our first priority. Jesus must always be the King in the throne room of our heart.

He is the best role model one can ever have! While God walked the earth, He shed forth examples of compassion, humility, praying faith, teaching, and boldness in the truth. In all that Jesus did, He made sure to include the disciples and answer their questions. Most of Jesus' answers to the disciples were not what they wanted to hear. How true that still is today!

In John 14, Jesus presented a revelation of who He really is to the disciples and what His plans were for them:

"Let not your heart be troubled: ye believe in God, believe also in me. In my Father's house are many mansions: if it were not so, I would have told you. I go to prepare a place for you. And if I go and prepare a place for you, I will come again, and receive you unto myself; that where I am, there ye may be also. And whither I go ye know, and the way ye know" (John 14:1-4).

King Jesus spoke about always being there for the disciples and that He was going to prepare a place in heaven for them. One disciple, Thomas, did not seem to understand:

"Thomas saith unto him, Lord, we know not whither thou goest; and how can we know the way? Jesus saith unto him, I am the way, the truth, and the life: no man cometh unto the Father, but by me. If ye had known me, ye should have known my Father also: and from henceforth ye know him, and have seen him" (John 14:5-7).

Jesus was giving a self-revelation; Jesus was in fact God in the flesh. He wanted the disciples to understand whom they were serving. Yet in verse 8, we see another disciple speak up with another question. They were not getting what Jesus was trying to teach them:

"Philip saith unto him, Lord, shew us the Father, and it sufficeth us. Jesus saith unto him, Have I been so long time with you, and yet hast thou not known me, Philip? he that hath seen me hath seen the Father; and how sayest thou then, Shew us the Father? Believest thou not that I am in the Father, and the Father in me? the words that I speak unto you I speak not of myself: but the Father that dwelleth in me, he doeth the works. Believe me that I am in the Father, and the Father in me: or else believe me for the very works' sake. Verily, verily, I say unto you, He that believeth on me, the works that I do shall he do also; and greater works than these shall he do; because I go unto my Father. And whatsoever ye shall ask in my name, that will I do, that the Father may be glorified in the Son. If ye shall ask any thing in my name, I will do it. If ye love me, keep my commandments" (John 14:8-15).

Jesus wanted them to understand who He really is, whom they were following. After the Lord spoke about the oneness of the Father and the Son, He told them that if they loved Him, to keep His commandments.

In order to be a proper Palace Keeper, in order to keep the commandments of the King, you must first know and learn who the King really is. When you get to know the King better and develop a closer relationship with Him, you begin to know His ways and understand them. So when it comes time for the King to direct your tasks, you will know the manner of His heart and your heart can respond properly. It will become easier to obey the Lord when He directs your daily job responsibilities. This will give you the King's favor, and you will be rewarded greatly.

Just like the disciples, it is easy to have inward challenges when Jesus brings forth something for us to do. *Am I good enough? Do I have what it takes? Will I fail or succeed? How do I know what to do and if it's right?*

These inward thoughts and fears are things that make us focus on the situation as if it were a problem and not on a solution to get the job done. As a Palace Keeper, the feeling can be overwhelming. God will never give you anything that you cannot handle. He will equip you with the right tools and show you how to use them.

Through Jesus' example and written Word, the Lord will teach you how to turn those inward challenges into stepping stones of victory!

Chapter 8: The Power of Influence

Tears stung my eyes as I lay there. I had to ask myself *How did I get here?* but the minute I did, I knew my answer. It started about five years before that point, when I met a boy. Of course, the typical things started to happen. Sweaty palms, butterfly bellies, and googly eyes.

I know now that it is never okay to put a person as a priority before God, for that is when being emotionally impure can happen. Just like Jessica did in the example I gave you earlier, I had put a guy where God was supposed to be in my heart. I had a boy as my idol. Oh, but he was *really* cute. All my friends thought so, too. That seed was planted and took me down a long road of pain, guilt, and heartbreak. That is one thing I can say that can be very damaging to a young person's life, especially mine at the time. **Influence.** We have all been given the power of influence.

Here's a perfect example for us, ladies. In the Garden of Eden, Eve influenced Adam to eat the forbidden fruit that God instructed them not to eat. In the Book of Genesis, God warned Adam not to eat the fruit of the Tree of Good and Evil. Better yet, God *commanded* Adam not to:

"And the LORD God commanded the man, saying, Of every tree of the garden thou mayest freely eat: but of the tree of the knowledge of good and evil, thou shalt not eat of it: for in the day that thou eatest thereof thou shalt surely die" (Genesis 2:16-17).

But if we skip to Genesis 3, we see that Eve was tempted into eating the fruit, and what's worse, she gave the fruit to her husband:

"And when the woman saw that the tree was good for food, and that it was pleasant to the eyes, and a tree to be desired to make one wise, she took of the fruit thereof, and did eat, and gave also unto her husband with her; and he did eat" (Genesis 3:6).

Scripture also tells us that Eve did know that the fruit was not good! Adam had shared with her what the Lord told him. He just didn't stand up to his authority position to stop it, but allowed Eve to influence the sin:

"And the woman said unto the serpent, We may eat of the fruit of the trees of the garden: but of the fruit of the tree which is in the midst of the garden, God hath said, Ye shall not eat of it, neither shall ye touch it, lest ye die" (Genesis 3:2-3).

As young ladies and growing women, the Lord has given us a special power of influence to use for His glory, not our own. Guarding our emotions will re-evaluate our motives and intentions behind our words and actions. This will leave the door open for Jesus to change our heart accordingly and not leave our heart open to unwanted thoughts and negativity.

The Scripture states that the fruit was "pleasant to the eyes." *Which pair of eyes was the Scripture talking about?* Eve's eyes were deceitful. The serpent influenced Eve to eat and planted that seed into her heart. Once she saw what she *"wanted,"* she thought it best to share with her husband and influenced him to partake in the sin. Though it was Adam's responsibility as her husband to have stopped this event before it happened, it was also the power of a woman's influence that overpowered God's word in Adam's heart.

"Discretion shall preserve thee, understanding shall keep thee" (Proverbs 2:11).

As females, we have more power than we know what to do with. If we can learn to lean on Jesus and allow Him to use that influence to enrich His kingdom, just think how many hearts we can reach!

In society today, we see the negative effects of a woman's influence. Instead of using her body for God's glory, she has exploited it to curve men's attention to herself. Instead of using her words for pleasant admirations, she speaks foul language and uses conniving attitudes to fulfill material desires. This is not how the King wants His daughters to act.

"To deliver thee from the strange woman, even from the stranger which flattereth with her words; which forsaketh the guide of her youth, and forgetteth the covenant of her God. For her house inclineth unto death, and her paths unto the dead" (Proverbs 2:16-18).
In the Book of Proverbs, we are warned of the ways in which not to act. What is more, gentlemen are expected not to give in to such women. Not just to avoid giving in physically, but also emotionally. God cares about men's emotional states just as much a woman's. The Scripture is clear that young men must also work on guarding their hearts as well. Yes, ladies, men do have hearts!

"My son, attend unto my wisdom, and bow thine ear to my understanding: that thou mayest regard discretion, and that thy lips may keep knowledge. For the lips of a strange woman drop as a honeycomb, and her mouth is smoother than oil: but her end is bitter as wormwood, sharp as a two-edged sword. Her feet go down to death; her steps take hold on hell. Lest thou shouldest ponder the path of life, her ways are moveable, that thou canst not know them. Hear me now therefore, O ye children, and depart not from the words of my mouth. Remove thy way far from her, and come not nigh the door of her house" (Proverbs 5:1-8).

Gentlemen, you are not exempt. You have a different kind of power of influence. While a woman more than likely uses her influence to manipulate others to do what she wants, you on the other hand are more bold and strong. The most attractive part of the power of influence for you is that first word, *"power."*

A perfect example is Jacob using his power of influence to gain the birthright from his twin and older brother, Esau. Esau was only older by like two seconds, but here's the deal: first-born sons in those days were supposed to get a special blessing from their father. This could include giving them all of the father's possessions and livestock. It could mean land and also money.

Basically, it was a very honorable blessing, one that Jacob managed to buy with one sorry bowl of soup. Jacob was always jealous of his brother. Even as they were in the womb, they fought and their mother Rebekah was confused:

"And the children struggled together within her; and she said, If it be so, why am I thus? And she went to inquire of the LORD. And the LORD said unto her, Two nations are in thy womb, and two manner of people shall be separated from thy bowels; and the one people shall be stronger than the other people; and the elder shall serve the younger. And when her days to be delivered were fulfilled, behold, there were twins in her womb. And the first came out red, all over like an hairy garment; and they called his name Esau. And after that came his brother out, and his hand took hold on Esau's heel; and his name was called Jacob: and Isaac was threescore years old when she bare them" (Genesis 25:22-26).

There came a point when they grew up and Jacob was preparing some stew or soup. Esau, a cunning hunter, came from the field and was faint. So, naturally, he asked his younger brother for some of the food:

"And Jacob sod pottage: and Esau came from the field, and he was faint: and Esau said to Jacob, Feed me, I pray thee, with that same red pottage; for I am faint" (Genesis 25:29-30).

Jacob seized the opportunity to use his power of influence on his brother!

"And Jacob said, Sell me this day thy birthright. And Esau said, Behold, I am at the point to die: and what profit shall this birthright do to me? And Jacob said, Swear to me this day; and he sware unto him: and he sold his birthright unto Jacob. Then Jacob gave Esau bread and pottage of lentiles; and he did eat and drink, and rose up, and went his way: thus Esau despised his birthright" (Genesis 25:31-34).

This "power of influence" is a powerful tool, and if the heart has wrong intentions, it can cause some deadly damage. With actions and words, a message is sent to the other person. Verbally and non-verbally, we are given power to influence our world. *How will you use it?*

Palace Keeper, protecting your emotional purity is only half of the process. You must also be careful not to influence others in a way that will lead them to emotional impurity. Through this power, great things can happen for our Father's kingdom. Lives can be changed and hearts mended if we properly use the power of influence well. At the same token, if we abuse that power, lives can be driven away from the King, and hearts will be left broken.

Ladies and gentlemen, boys and girls, look around you. *What do you see?* I bet when you look at one another, meaning someone around your age, you don't necessarily picture him or her as a brother or sister in Christ. *Why not?* The terms "brother and sister" respect a person's role that he or she has in God's kingdom.

The purity of your heart is not only going to keep you from stumbling, but it is also designed to help your fellow brothers and sisters in Christ. This is a form of respect to them. The terms "brother" and "sister" are not reserved for the elders of the church. It's more than that, just like the purity of your entire palace will affect the decisions of all your fellow brothers and sisters. Romans 14:13 tells us:

"Let us not therefore judge one another any more: but judge this rather, that no man put a stumblingblock or an occasion to fall in his brother's way."

Point blank: don't use your power of influence to make your brother or sister stumble! Be mindful that your fellow brothers and sisters are also in need of being their Palace Keepers. Help them succeed by being respectful to their emotional purity. Watch your language and actions.

Ladies, are you treating your fellow brothers like sons of the King, or are they just names on your crush list? Gentlemen, are you treating your fellow sisters in Christ like princesses of purity, or are they only something pretty to look at? Don't spread around your emotional baggage! We all have plenty of our own, thank you.

When you emotionally attach yourself to your fellow brothers and sisters, especially when it's more than one at a time, this becomes not only a stumbling block for your purity but for theirs as well. Not allowing God to filter your emotions will make it difficult for you to see that person the way God wants you to. Instead of seeing them as a son or daughter of the King, your emotions will pigeonhole that one into being the hero of your fantasy love story.

Let's turn those stumbling-blocks into stepping stones of victory! Can you imagine, if we all started acknowledging and treating one another like brothers and sisters in Christ, with respect and conscious minds of purity, how far we could go together to do God's work?

Chapter 9: The Spectator or the Participant

Opportunity:
A good chance for advancement or progress

When Jesus walked on the water, Peter took a step of faith and followed Him. Peter did walk on the water, too, until he looked down. You know, most of the time we are our worst enemies. Even when the blessing is right in front of our faces, we tend to let fear creep into our hearts and steal our hope. We cannot make progress or advancement in our lives by looking at our feet or what is beneath them. *What good will that do our perception? How will we be able to see where we are headed if we are too busy focusing on the path beneath us?*

Peter became fearful. He was fearful at seeing the waves, the troubles, and the problems. Peter began sinking in doubt. He gave in to his humanity, his inevitable feeling of inadequacy. In Peter's mind, he knew that no human could really walk on water. He knew it was physically impossible for man to have that kind of ability on this earth. The physics did not match. Yet Peter knew in his mind that Jesus was no ordinary man. He was not just the Messiah but God Himself in the flesh.

Peter knew that with Jesus, our God, all things were possible and he stepped out, not because he felt that he could do it by his own abilities; by man's abilities. Peter knew the man who was walking on the water in front of him was God, and Peter could do anything as long as he followed Jesus! He would be with God! When Peter began sinking, in a quick moment Jesus reached out with an opportunity for Peter, a good chance to progress! He offered His hand to Peter, a way up from the water and a way out of the waves. Jesus offered him help.

"And Peter answered him and said, Lord, if it be thou, bid me come unto thee on the water. And he said, Come. And when Peter was come down out of the ship, he walked on the water, to go to Jesus. But when he saw the wind boisterous, he was afraid; and beginning to sink, he cried, saying, Lord, save me. And immediately Jesus stretched forth his hand, and caught him, and said unto him, O thou of little faith, wherefore didst thou doubt?" (Matthew 14:28-31).

We have a choice. We can continue sinking in our doubt, pouting our life away like a child sent to bed early, or we can accept the opportunity to progress. We can accept that good chance of survival. Here's a scenario for you:

If you were stranded on an island by yourself, with no food or water for ten days and knew after those ten days you would die, what would you do? Sit back and enjoy the mini vacation! Get a sweet tan!

Maybe, but after the first day, you would start to realize the severity of the situation. By the third day, you'd feel hungry, and your stomach would start cramping. By the sixth day, your mentality would start to deteriorate, and you would see illusions.

You may even start telling yourself that people are coming the next day to take you to Red Lobster. Your body weakens even more the ninth day. You feel the cold of the ocean breeze more on your exposed being. You may even say to yourself that help will not come now.

After hearing these circumstances, what do you think the outcome of the tenth day will be? *Victory?* When we are not guarding our hearts, we become lazy and comfortable on our own little island. Even though we know that we need to get up and do something, we make the choice to sit and whine. We love to throw "pity parties" and invite everyone we know to join.

The more we ignore the fact that our hearts need help, the more we lose out on the victory. We must first step out of the boat in order to reach the opportunities the Lord has for us. God sets things up so we have to turn to Him in order to achieve victory over trials. If Peter never stepped out, what kind of man would he have turned out to be? *Would Peter have been a spectator of the miracle and not a participant?*

To be a **spectator** is to be someone on the sidelines, just like the other disciples on the boat. They just watched this amazing miracle but were not part of it. It is someone who just watches from afar as everything unfolds.

Sometimes being a spectator is a good thing if the situation calls for it. In the case of emotional impurity, being a spectator can actually slow the cleansing process. It really requires someone to take *action*. To take action in a situation, you are no longer a spectator, or a watcher. You become a **participant**. You become Peter, taking action by stepping out and making his way closer to Jesus.

I know deep in my soul I want to *participate* in what God is doing! *Don't you?* Not just a spectator of a miracle, I want to be involved in one, especially in my own heart. The job as a Palace Keeper cannot be fulfilled correctly if there is no action. I never heard of a good guard who just stood while thieves raided the palace. It is about stepping up to what is being asked of you to preserve what God has given you.

How can we possibly help others if we don't first take that opportunity to step out on faith, trust God, and allow Him to change our motives? God will still use you even if you're not perfectly put together. He is God and has all control. However, our emotional purity is left in our hands so that we may make the right decisions. *Will we take the opportunity to claim the victory of purity? Or will we allow impurity to wash over our heart?*

Peter chose life! If Peter was a Palace Keeper, do you think he would be a spectator or a participant? I don't think Peter would just sit on the sidelines as the waves washed over him. I also don't think Peter would be the type of guard who would be leaning against the wall, arms folded, and whistling while thieves raided the palace of its treasures. We need to participate in the process toward pure success and not be the spectator of our emotional downfall.

I've done this so many times. It's hard not to just cry to the Lord, *"Jesus, please give me the strength!"* and think He will "magically" sprinkle from heaven some strengthening fairy dust. Our God is not a God of illusion. He is, however, a provider to those who diligently seek Him. He will provide for us an opportunity to be strong in Him.

"But without faith it is impossible to please him: for he that cometh to God must believe that he is, and that he is a rewarder of them that diligently seek him" (Hebrews 11:6).

The circumstances of our situation to progress will not always be easy. If the Lord never puts trials in our lives, if we are never challenged in areas where we need strength, how will we be better individually? Truth is, we wouldn't be. *How can we learn from something that has no challenge?*

I've never really known people who were born with a silver spoon in their mouths to spit it out. When someone inherits millions of dollars, you rarely hear him say, "No thanks! I'm content." Think about that spiritually. If God made it easy for us to serve Him, what would that ultimate purpose be for? Or think about it this way, if King Jesus gave us all silver-spoon blessings in all areas of our lives, what would we have to look forward to? We would already have everything we *think* we need. I feel we would never give God the time of day because we have everything perfect. *Why would we need God if we have everything we already want?*

It is important to thank Him for the good and the bad opportunities of progress. A bad opportunity of progress means that we are progressing backward. If we see our hearts going back, not forward, we need to recognize that it is an opportunity to grow and thank God for it while taking action to turn it around. Thank Him for showing us the areas of weakness, and ask for His guidance to get on the right track of progression.

Chapter 10: Proverbs 4:23 Study

Much like jobs in the real world, God has many jobs for us in the spiritual world. There are many jobs throughout Scripture, but one of the most crucial jobs in all God's Word is the guard of your heart. This is what I've been calling a "Palace Keeper."

If that job is not filled by the right applicant, there is no telling what condition your heart will be in. Just like a job on earth, an interview process needs to be implemented before we give any job responsibilities to someone else. *Is this person going to take care of my heart the way it needs to? What are their motives for wanting my heart? I really need a full-time guard, but will this person only act part time? Will this person be healthy or unhealthy for my heart?*

I want you for a moment to read the verse of Scripture below, and ask God to reveal its truth to your heart so you will understand the job of guarding it.

"Keep thy heart with all diligence; for out of it are the issues of life" (Proverbs 4:23).

When you are looking for a new job, aren't there questions concerning the job that are important to you? Like: *What kind of job is it? How will I perform the tasks asked of me? Why is this job needed?* It's all about the what, how, and why.

The *when* isn't really important because we already know the answer to that: If we are searching for a job, *when* do we need one? Right now!

Those three questions can apply to three parts of
Scripture:
1.) What is the Lord trying to say to me and teach me?
[the topic]
2.) How can I properly follow what the Lord says?
[our response]
3.) Why is the Lord bringing this to my attention?
[the lesson]

All three of these questions need to be looked at carefully and prayed about. Each one leads into the next one and will reveal many things to your heart that God wants you to know. Many passages of Scripture are instructions on how to keep our hearts pure and solely dependent on Jesus. In order to properly analyze what job is required of us through Proverbs 4:23, we must allow God to interview us. We cannot just read about a job in the newspaper and then start working the next day, right? There has to be a "cleansing" process of different applicants before the right one is chosen. If we take that same concept, there has to be a "cleansing" process in our hearts in order to properly fulfill what is asked of us. This verse in Proverbs will help us all to see the "what," "how," and the "why" in God's plan for our hearts. Then that God will lead us to the right paths to true emotional healing and purity.

Part #1: <u>What</u> is our main job requirement?

Keep thy heart . . .

"Keep" is such a powerful word! We can start to study this verse by finding the definition for the word "keep."

Keep:
to hold/retain; maintain in condition/order; to maintain control of/ to guard or protect

The Scripture states that we need to "keep" or guard our hearts. It is just too easy to let things slowly trickle inside our seams because many things that are disguised as good are really not.

"Beware of false prophets, which come to you in sheep's clothing, but inwardly they are ravening wolves" (Matthew 7:15).

Guarding your heart is a full-time job, just like that of a guard who protects a beautiful palace. It is his job not to allow anyone inside the palace who is not authorized. If the guard is not diligent, treasures and valuable items may be stolen from the palace. The owners of high estate who reside there will not be safe if they have a guard who is sleeping on the job or is not careful. Lives may even be in danger.

Think about your heart as that beautiful palace. God is the owner, but you have been given the job of the full-time guard.
What does God expect from you as a guard? What must you be alert about to protect the palace? What treasures has God given you to watch over? Though we may have the heart in our possession, it still belongs to the Creator.

"For if there be first a willing mind, it is accepted according to that a man hath, and not according to that he hath not" (II Corinthians 8:12).

Part of doing a good job is having a willing mind, meaning a conscience that will surrender. Our hearts need to be willing as well to allow God to change us. It is only through a willing mind and heart that the Lord really can move. Though the Almighty has all power and authority and can perform this instantly, He would rather have us make the right choice in choosing His way. If you are unwilling to allow God to change your heart, God will not stop trying to reach you. He will, however, patiently wait on the sidelines for you to notice what you are missing. Having a full-time job as our Palace Keeper, we must be willing to complete what is asked of us. If we are not, we are just stagnant and useless workers.

"If ye be willing and obedient, ye shall eat the good of the land" (Isaiah 1:19).

In order to fully understand the process of guarding our hearts, we will have to look at the next part of the verse. Now that we know what the job is, how can we accomplish what is required?

Part #2: How do we do the job that is required?

. . . with all diligence . . .

Diligence:
a zealous and careful nature in one's
actions and work.

Okay, so we have gone through the first part of the interview process. *How do you think it is going? Do you think you will be able to accomplish the tasks asked of you? How do you feel about your abilities to be a Palace Peeper? A little overwhelmed?*

Here's the good news: God offers free training! That's right, it's free. You do not have to pay a thing. He has already paid full price up front. God is the only One who understands the full capacity of what it takes to guard a heart. He is the only One who knows the ins and outs of the job and how to prepare us for the journey. Being the Creator and owner of the heart, Jesus is the absolute best source to seek for help as to how to do your job well.

Think about this scenario. *If you are supposed to be a palace guard and have a question about your job, would you ask the gardener? How about the nanny? The cook?*

It just doesn't make sense to ask someone about a job that they know nothing about. There will be co-workers who will try to influence your job decisions, but the right choices have to come from someone who has the knowledge. That someone is the Lord Jesus Christ, the King of kings!

We all are in charge of making sure our hearts stay guarded and protected. It is a daily process, one that requires absolute precaution and carefulness. To be diligent is to be consistent, constantly filtering what goes in and out of your heart, much like a guard constantly filtering what goes in and out of a palace.

Palace Keeper, the best filter is the Lord Jesus Christ, and putting Him in that rightful place will make the diligent process possible. He has the knowledge and wisdom to know how to filter your heart yet has given you the opportunity to receive the knowledge and wisdom through the Scriptures.

"And the scripture was fulfilled which saith, Abraham believed God, and it was imputed unto him for righteousness: and he was called the Friend of God" (James 2:23).

In an earthly job, we usually try to please the boss, right? Now, I didn't say the boss was easy to please, but we are in luck. As the King of our palace, God is merciful and full of grace. Hallelujah! Scriptures describe the type of boss the Lord Jesus is but also tell us that He is more than just our boss to please. He is also our Savior, our Father, and our Friend. How many bosses do you know have all those qualities?

"For the LORD God is a sun and shield: the LORD will give grace and glory: no good thing will he withhold from them that walk uprightly" (Psalm 84:11).

"There is no God else beside me; a just God and a Saviour; there is none beside me" (Isaiah 45:21).

So we looked at the first two parts: The "what" (*keep thy heart*) and the "how" (*with all diligence*). We understand now that with emotional impurity, the main problem starts in our hearts, and it is our responsibility to properly guard it, as appointed by the Lord. Now that we see this, we need to know *why* we are doing this and what God expects as results.

Part #3: <u>Why</u> do we need to have this job?

. . . for out of it are the issues of life.

Take a second and think about why you would need a full-time job. *Why are you searching? Is it because you need to have a steady income, or are you just bored?* For many of us, we are not given much of a choice when it comes to not having a full-time job. In order to live decently, we must have some sort of financial stability, and having a full-time job provides that. Some households are blessed to have just one working spouse, while others need both to work in order to make ends meet. Neither is wrong or right; it is based upon the different needs of the family. *What are your needs?* We'll get back to this soon.

Throughout the Bible we can plainly see how God feels about our hearts and that He cares about what is inside them. It is not just Proverbs 4:23 alone that deal with this issue.

An **issue** means a situation or a problem surrounding a specific circumstance. It is more of a conflicting situation, which may involve one or more parties. *"The issues of life"* can mean all possible situations that our hearts can create or lead us into. Instead of saying "for out of it", we can also say "for out of your heart." It means just the same. An issue doesn't necessarily have to be seen as negative. There can be many positive issues; however, it all depends on the state of our heart and what we are feeding it.

127

"Let the words of my mouth, and the meditation of my heart, be acceptable in thy sight, O LORD, my strength, and my redeemer" (Psalm 19:14).

"For there is no faithfulness in their mouth; their inward part is very wickedness; their throat is an open sepulchre; they flatter with their tongue" (Psalm 5:9).

We have to wonder why emotional purity is so important to God. We have heard many times that our physical bodies should be kept pure; however, there is not much emphasis in Christian society about the emotional and spiritual conditions of our hearts. I have found through my research and prayer something that is quite profound. I can also see it in my own life by some of my past choices.

When it comes to physical purity, the decision to be kept pure needs to be made prior to any awkward or uncomfortable encounters. It is more important to prepare yourself *before* the temptation than to be unprepared and vulnerable to fall. I believe that Proverbs 4:23 is the Lord warning us about this ahead of time.

For me, I see now how vulnerable and fragile my heart really was before I put the Lord first. I had allowed other people to be the king or boss of my heart, instead of putting God in that position. What was worse, I did not take the job of being my Palace Keeper but had given that away as well. My emotions were being controlled by other people who should never have had that kind of power. It is very dangerous to give your heart away before giving your body. Looking back now, I realize that I had moved things too soon and too fast. I was emotionally promiscuous. My decisions seemed like my decisions, but in actuality I had become a puppet with invisible strings.

Not protecting our hearts and our emotions is what actually leads us to do things we wouldn't normally do. It is rare for us just to wake up every day and purposely want to make those decisions that will send us down the wrong path. It is a constant battle with our natural desires to keep them in line every day with God's desires. We hold some precious treasures in our hearts, just like a palace. If someone has control over our emotional well-being, those treasures will not be cared for the way the Lord intended them to be.

In order to stay cautious and protect our hearts, we really need to keep God as our focus. Yes, that is easier said than done. The best part of having God as the boss of your heart is that you will always have an opportunity to grow! He has many lessons and skills to teach you and is always willing to help you throughout the process. Choosing a different path, meaning keeping your heart an open door and not putting up your guard, will only leave you feeling empty, hurt, depressed, unloved, and full of many other unpleasant but inevitable feelings. That is *"why"* it is truly important to protect your heart against emotional impurity.

We see the "what," "how," and "why."
What about the "when?"

"So will I sing praise unto thy name for ever, that I may daily perform my vows" (Psalm 61:8).

I asked God when I was first shown this pattern in the Scripture, "Where is the 'when' in all of this? When do I put this into action?" As I pondered this, the Lord began to reveal to me other verses for the answer.

It is **daily**! We must apply His principles to our lives each and every day for our hearts to be properly protected and changed. It is true that God's timing is perfect and things will happen when He ordains it. However, *now* is when we have to obey His Word and apply it.

"I protest by your rejoicing which I have in Christ Jesus our Lord, I die daily" (II Corinthians 15:31).
When I first read II Corinthians 15:31, I have to admit I did get a little freaked out. *What? Die daily? No, thank you!* But the more I read the passage and the surrounding verses, I began to see that Paul was talking about his humanity in the situation. It is about putting down what our flesh wants and picking up what God wants. Not just when we feel like it or when it is convenient, but all the time! It is protecting us emotionally so that physically we are protected as well.

"Now therefore hearken unto me, O ye children: for blessed are they that keep my ways. Hear instruction, and be wise, and refuse it not. Blessed is the man that heareth me, watching daily at my gates, waiting at the posts of my doors. For whoso findeth me findeth life, and shall obtain favour of the LORD" (Proverbs 8:32-35).

Okay, now remember earlier when I asked you what your needs were. After reading a bit more, did you find that most of what you considered your *"needs"* were actually your *"wants"*?

When we know who God is, we know what He wants us to do and we are able to keep our hearts diligent for Him. Our hearts then change and our wants become His wants.

Okay, Palace Keeper. You now understand what your job is, what is expected of you, and how to get the job done. King Jesus has hired you, and now it's show time!

Palace guard
—noun
1. the security force protecting a palace.
2. a group of trusted advisers who often control access to a sovereign, president, or other chief executive.

Being a palace guard is serious business. Your job is to protect and control access to a very important part of your life. Think about the guards at Buckingham Palace. *What if they slacked off on their jobs?* The queen could be in danger! When you think about being the Palace Keeper of your own heart, the ruler of it should be King Jesus Himself. God doesn't need your protection, but you preserve what He has given you. When you give your whole heart to God, it no longer belongs to you but to Him. So, even though you are protecting yourself, you are in turn respecting the King by doing so.

"Unto the pure all things are pure: but unto them that are defiled and unbelieving is nothing pure; but even their mind and conscience is defiled" (Titus 1:15).

"The heart is deceitful above all things, and desperately wicked: who can know it?" (Jeremiah 17:9).

The concept of someone guarding their heart became more complex to explain as I started piecing this book together. In the Scripture, Jesus constantly refers to the heart as the main place where His Spirit is to dwell when received and where we must obey Him and love Him. It soon became clear to me that to guard a heart involved more than the heart itself.

There are many avenues that good and bad influences take to get to our hearts. Hearts are naturally deceitful, and that is why we need a cleansing process. Opinions, motivations, and intentions are fed into us by our senses, and the final data resides in our heart. Even when receiving the beautiful gift of the Holy Ghost, it does not start from within. God must pour His Spirit from above, to our open hearts below. It's a vertical process which translates to how to we can guard ourselves.

"Every good gift and every perfect gift is from above, and cometh down from the Father of lights, with whom is no variableness, neither shadow of turning" (James 1:17).

How we translate our influences is a natural act. The only thing we have control over is controlling how much or how little something influences us. How far does an influence get? One way or another, we will be affected by everything we see, hear, touch, taste, or smell. We form memories and associate certain words with what we come in contact with.

We are made in such a magnificent way that without any effort on our part, our body can process data and characteristics surrounding that data to a full completion. This can be the work of our subconscious. When equipping ourselves with God's tools, the outcome is more positive and beneficial to us. We will get into what those tools are later.

Here is a list of some examples of good and bad influences that we may experience daily. An influence can be just about anything, and the most influences vary between different people. What may influence me, may not influence you. The most important part is to remember which influences please God and which ones don't. Now, take a look at the list. They ate listed in no particular order, but maybe you can relate to some:

GOOD INFLUENCES:
● **Godly parents/mentors**
● **Godly spouse**

- Pastor/Pastor's wife/Ministers/Youth leaders
- Church/Fellowship
- Love/Sincerity
- Scriptures

BAD INFLUENCES:
- Worldwide media
- Anger/Fear/Lust
- Rebellious friends
- Disobedience
- Perversion
- Pride

Influences vary from person to person. A girlfriend/boyfriend can be a great influence for someone, even walking him/her closer to the Lord. To another person, a relationship can take him or her down a long and hurtful path leading that one away from the King. It all depends on the heart of the influence. An influence does one of two things: *glorifies God or glorifies man.*

Think back to the earlier description of my picture of a palace. Try to imagine a big mansion or castle in real life. Different rooms and avenues all have a reason for being there. The same goes for our spiritual palaces. Let us break down those parts of a palace.

A *physical* palace has these five main parts:

Gate
Courtyard
Foyer
Throne Room
Grounds
A *spiritual* palace has these five main parts:

Mind
Thoughts
Decisions
Heart
Body

All these parts work together to shape the condition of our soul and all have a specific role to play when we are a Palace Keeper. If we compare the parts of a physical palace with the parts of the spiritual palace, we will see how they coincide. Now, let's look at each individually…

Gate:
a point of entry to a space enclosed by walls or an opening in a fence. Gates may prevent or control entry or exit, or they may be merely decorative.

When we are exposed to something through one of our five senses, the first reaction approaches our minds. This is the first step to guarding your palace properly. Once we recognize a thought or idea, it is at the gate of our mind. We can decide whether we want to let it in or not. *Do we want to think about it more or do we not?* The question we need to be asking is: *Does this thought or idea glorify God or does it offend Him?*

Our mind is where wisdom is supposed to dwell first and foremost. Proverbs 8 describes wisdom as having a voice that needs to be heard, that cries out at the gates:

Doth not wisdom cry? and understanding put forth her voice? She standeth in the top of high places, by the way in the places of the paths. She crieth at the gates, at the entry of the city, at the coming in at the doors. Unto you, O men, I call; and my voice is to the sons of man. O ye simple, understand wisdom: and, ye fools, be ye of an understanding heart. Hear; for I will speak of excellent things; and the opening of my lips shall be right things. For my mouth shall speak truth; and wickedness is an abomination to my lips. All the words of my mouth are in righteousness; there is nothing froward or perverse in them. They are all plain to him that understandeth, and right to them that find knowledge. Receive my instruction, and not silver; and knowledge rather than choice gold.

For wisdom is better than rubies; and all the things that may be desired are not to be compared to it (Proverbs 8:1-11).

We are instructed to have wisdom in understanding and knowledge at the gates of our minds. This will prepare us against wickedness and other things that are an abomination to the King. The gate of our minds must be active and not merely for decoration. *What is the point of having a mind if we don't use it for its intended purpose?* It is not just to acknowledge and process data; our minds need to discern data. God says that we have a responsibility to try the different influences that come our way.

"Beloved, believe not every spirit, but try the spirits whether they are of God: because many false prophets are gone out into the world" (I John 4:1).

Our minds are the gateway for influences to come in and go out. When we dismiss an influence that is trying to get in, we close the entrance. When we make the decision to think more about an influence, our minds open and we allow ourselves to think more on the subject. The influence then enters our gate and comes inside our courtyard.

The courtyard, or our thoughts, is the gathering place for all the influences that we have allowed inside the gate of our mind. Picture the courtyard as a busy and loud marketplace. In the early centuries, the courtyard of a castle was where people shopped, did business transactions, held trials, preached, or just mingled.

This was a place where vendors would lay out all their best merchandise, draping the finest linens over the front of their carts. The healthiest livestock was displayed on tabletops to entice passing eyes. Expensive gems and gold from overseas shined as the vendors waved them to the local damsels. Yes, the courtyard was a potluck of different things from around the world.

Depending on what good or bad influences you've allowed into the palace gates will determine whether the atmosphere of the courtyard is good or bad. That will determine how your thoughts and opinions will be formed. Within your thought process, there is a vulnerability factor. Due to the amount of influences that tend to flood your courtyard, it is easy to feel overwhelmed with all of the influences. It may get confusing as you consider what decision to make and where you stand in your thinking about a subject.

"For the wicked boasteth of his heart's desire, and blesseth the covetous, whom the LORD abhorreth. The wicked, through the pride of his countenance, will not seek after God: God is not in all his thoughts" (Psalm 10:3-4).

Many times, influences that seemed good at the gate change for the worse once inside. It is our job to spot those bad apples right away and throw them out! If we don't, they can cause chaos and destruction to our thoughts. Bad influences will try their best to corrupt our thinking and manipulate a way into the interior of the castle, the interior of our heart.

Good influences are like good townspeople. They may want to pay their respects to the king, maybe even dine with him. Meanwhile, bad influences are like town thieves and are just interested in taking from the king and don't respect him at all.

This is why we must discern what is bumbling about in our minds. Our thoughts should glorify God and His ways. They should be pleasing to the King and far from wickedness. Our thoughts need to be in line with the King's because He knows what is best:

"For my thoughts are not your thoughts, neither are your ways my ways, saith the LORD" (Isaiah 55:8).

The interior of the castle is where the heart is. It is where royalty lives and where all the decisions are made. Once inside those walls, influences must travel through your conscience before getting to your heart. Your conscience can be seen as **the foyer** of a palace. The foyer will have many doors, hallways, and stairs. It is a vestibule of entrances and exits. Spiritually speaking, this part is a vestibule of decisions. Many ways will seem to be the right way but are not. It is your own decision as to whether that influence will continue into your heart or be dismissed from your palace.

This is a crucial point of the process. It is this foyer of our conscience where we make decisions that will affect our hearts either positively or negatively.

Our palaces have many hidden tunnels and hallways that we don't even know about. There are some doors we cannot open without a specific key and other doors are always unlocked. Some stairs lead to dark dungeons and others into beautiful sunrooms. Some hallways will lead to a maze of walls and floors that can cause confusion. Other hallways lead to glorious rooms and balconies overlooking the gorgeous surrounding landscape.

There is one room that is marveled by all who come to respect the king of the palace. This room shines like spun gold in high sunlight. It bursts with radiance and echoes exaltation. The silence in this room is due to heartfelt worship and honor. It is the room where the highest throne is placed and where the king greets his subjects. Just a few people will appreciate the magnitude of power and love that fills the air.

This is called the **throne room**. It contains the crown that is either loved or despised. The beauty of this room can only be appreciated with willingness. Negative influences will move quickly and sneakily through the palace with no regard to the king's rules or policy. They will *never* approach the throne room. They lack respect for the crown. Selfishness and greed drive them, and they keep stealing, feeding from, and mooching off the King. The throne room to them is a threat.

As the Palace Keeper, if you're not careful, they could overpower you and run wild. With many hidden tunnels and hallways, there's no telling where they will hide or what they will take from the King. Tearing down what the King has built is humorous and delightful to them. You will be affected greatly, and so will your relationship with the King.

However, if we've allowed into our palace positive influences, they will always be willing and anxious to approach the throne room. Humble and meek in spirit, they will wait for you to guide them to the King. They will yield to instruction and/or correction. They have the upmost respect for their King and will fall on their faces before His throne. They show no hesitation to bow or kneel, for their honor is to pay respect to the Almighty King. What the King wants is their focus, and with their whole being, they will build up the palace and provide good works. In turn, they will have respect for you and your job as a Palace Keeper.

They would not want your relationship with the King to suffer and will be patient with your requests.

The throne room is where the King needs to dwell in order to properly maintain the whole palace. As the Palace Keeper, it is our job to protect and honor the King. It may be our very lives that depend on that the most. The types of influences you've allowed into your mind, thoughts, decisions, and heart will ultimately determine the quality of this last part of your palace.

The grounds, or your body, speak volumes of the quality of the Palace Keeper. As you do your job, if you do it well and have only allowed good influences to come in, your grounds will be classy, clean, and taken care of well. However, if you've slacked on your job or have made bad choices in which influences have entered, your grounds suffer, and this is evident by the amount of garbage or litter that taints the beautiful exterior.

Protecting our bodies goes deeper than just keeping everything nice and pretty. Just like taking care of the grounds or landscaping of a glorious palace, workers provide hard labor and know-how as to what it takes not only to make the grounds stunning but to also maintain the quality. To take care of and maintain the purity of our bodies, inside and outside, we have to be careful what influences our decisions and our hearts. King Jesus wants us to keep our body as a clean temple for His Spirit. Like a king of a palace, the appearance *and* value of the grounds make him happy.

This means more than just waiting until you're married to have sex; it's also being careful not to put toxins in your body, as well as not altering the exterior and changing God's perfect work.

146

"Meats for the belly, and the belly for meats: but God shall destroy both it and them. Now the body is not for fornication, but for the Lord; and the Lord for the body. And God hath both raised up the Lord, and will also raise up us by his own power.

Know ye not that your bodies are the members of Christ? shall I then take the members of Christ, and make them the members of an harlot? God forbid. What? know ye not that he which is joined to an harlot is one body? for two, saith he, shall be one flesh. But he that is joined unto the Lord is one spirit.

Flee fornication. Every sin that a man doeth is without the body; but he that committeth fornication sinneth against his own body. What? know ye not that your body is the temple of the Holy Ghost which is in you, which ye have of God, and ye are not your own?For ye are bought with a price: therefore glorify God in your body, and in your spirit, which are God's (I Corinthians 6:13-20).

All these parts—our mind, thoughts, decisions, heart, and body—make up our palace. Protecting the purity of our heart is a big job because we have to guard and watch over everything. These parts will affect how pure our heart is in the end. Even though it is a big job, God has already setup tools for you to get the job done, and get it done well.

Chapter 12: Tools of a Palace Keeper - Summary

We all know the importance of a clean home. It is a vital and healthy environment for our family and for us. Part of being clean is being uncluttered. I can say with confidence that our dining room table has become a "catch all" for things. Most days we never get to the piles, and they become a decoration. We can't even use the dining room table for its real purpose!

God sees our hearts in that same condition. It is vital and healthy to have a heart that is clean. We not only have to be in charge of what goes in and out of our hearts, but we must also maintain what is already inside. Every day, we allow influences to pile up and need to take care of them properly.

We must organize or throw away these influences. If we don't, the piles grow higher and higher. The longer we wait to de-clutter, the more difficult the process will be. Soon, there will be no more room and our hearts cannot be used for their intended purpose.

As a Palace Keeper, you have certain tools given to you by the King of kings so you can do your job well. Let's take a closer look at the list below and then look at each tool individually.

This list shows us the tools to use when we are being a Palace Keeper. The next ten chapters will go into more detail about each one individually.

- **The Word**
- **Prayer**
- **Faith**
- **Repentance**
- **Baptism**
- **Holy Ghost**
- **Obedience**
- **Discernment**
- **Proper fellowship**
- **Standards**

Chapter 13: Tools of a Palace Keeper- The Word

Okay, first day on the job as a Palace Keeper! You have been through orientation and now know the five parts of the palace you will have to guard. You have your instructions from the King and your list of tools to do the job superbly, but you're a little nervous. There are a lot of aspects to your job, and you don't know where to start. No one has even trained you on how to use the tools yet! You look around the palace and realize, *Wow, there is so much work to do!* You reach into your bag and pull out the living Word.

The Word, or the Bible, will tell you how to protect the gate of your mind, the courtyard of your influences, the foyer of your decisions, how to place King Jesus always in the throne room of your heart and maintain the grounds of your body.

God's Word is by far the best tool that you can ever have! It is the most essential part of your walk with the Lord and will help you organize things in your life. The decisions you make and how you react to them can be guided by Scripture daily.

In Matthew 21:42-44, Jesus spoke to the chief priests and elders of the Temple:

"Did ye never read in the scriptures, The stone which the builders rejected, the same is become the head of the corner: this is the Lord's doing, and it is marvellous in our eyes? Therefore say I unto you, The kingdom of God shall be taken from you, and given to a nation bringing forth the fruits thereof. And whosoever shall fall on this stone shall be broken: but on whomsoever it shall fall, it will grind him to powder."

Jesus was telling them that Scripture confirms the power of the Lord. In today's society, it is getting more and more difficult to see examples of people following the Word. They don't seem to understand the great tool Scripture can be. What is worse, as the generations pass, we seem to be less rooted in the Scriptures. The Lord said, "The stone which the builders rejected." God's Word is a foundation for your entire palace. It is the stone to stand firmly upon, and when faced with troubles, we can hold to it. *If you reject the very stone that can create a solid foundation, how steady can you really expect that foundation to be?*

In Luke 6:48-49, Jesus gave us an example of a solid foundation. We read this earlier, but the great thing about Scripture is you can read it over and over, and it will continue ministering:

"He is like a man which built an house, and digged deep, and laid the foundation on a rock: and when the flood arose, the stream beat vehemently upon that house, and could not shake it: for it was founded upon a rock. But he that heareth, and doeth not, is like a man that without a foundation built an house upon the earth; against which the stream did beat vehemently, and immediately it fell; and the ruin of that house was great."

Being the Palace Keeper, you have to be constantly aware of what is going on to protect yourself. God's written Word will help you along the way. It will also show you who King Jesus really is and give you confidence in your knowledge of Him. To have a good and solid foundation, you have to know the King whom you are serving. *What is His personality? What are His likes and dislikes? Who is He really?* These answers can be found in the Bible.

Our God is the Lord Jesus Christ. There is only one God, and He is the King of all that you see and don't see. He has all power and is almighty in His reign. What He says, He will do but in His time. He is the Creator of the earth and the heavens, and He is the beginning and the end. The fullness of the Godhead dwells in Jesus. Open up God's Word with me, and let us read some passages that will confirm the King's identity:

"In the beginning was the Word, and the Word was with God, and the Word was God. The same was in the beginning with God. All things were made by him; and without him was not any thing made that was made" (John 1:1-3).

"And the Word was made flesh, and dwelt among us, (and we beheld his glory, the glory as of the only begotten of the Father,) full of grace and truth" (John 1:14).

"For unto us a child is born, unto us a son is given: and the government shall be upon his shoulder: and his name shall be called Wonderful, Counseller, The mighty God, The everlasting Father, The Prince of Peace" (Isaiah 9:6).

"Ye are my witnesses, saith the LORD, and my servant whom I have chosen: that ye may know and believe me, and understand that I am he: before me there was no God formed, neither shall there be after me. I, even I, am the LORD; and beside me there is no saviour. I have declared, and have saved, and I have shewed, when there was no strange god among you: therefore ye are my witnesses, saith the LORD, that I am God" (Isaiah 43:10-12).

"There is one body, and one Spirit, even as ye are called in one hope of your calling; one Lord, one faith, one baptism, one God and Father of all, who is above all, and through all, and in you all" (Ephesians 4:4-6).

"That their hearts might be comforted, being knit together in love, and unto all riches of the full assurance of understanding, to the acknowledgement of the mystery of God, and of the Father, and of Christ; in whom are hid all the treasures of wisdom and knowledge. And this I say, lest any man should beguile you with enticing words. For though I be absent in the flesh, yet am I with you in the spirit, joying and beholding your order, and the stedfastness of your faith in Christ. As ye have therefore received Christ Jesus the Lord, so walk ye in him: rooted and built up in him, and stablished in the faith, as ye have been taught, abounding therein with thanksgiving. Beware lest any man spoil you through philosophy and vain deceit, after the tradition of men, after the rudiments of the world, and not after Christ. For in him dwelleth all the fulness of the Godhead bodily" (Colossians 2:2-9).

"For this is good and acceptable in the sight of God our Saviour; who will have all men to be saved, and to come unto the knowledge of the truth. For there is one God, and one mediator between God and men, the man Christ Jesus; who gave himself a ransom for all, to be testified in due time" (I Timothy 2:3-6).

"That thou keep this commandment without spot, unrebukeable, until the appearing of our Lord Jesus Christ: which in his times he shall shew, who is the blessed and only Potentate, the King of kings, and Lord of lords; who only hath immortality, dwelling in the light which no man can approach unto; whom no man hath seen, nor can see: to whom be honour and power everlasting" (I Timothy 6:14-16).

"For the grace of God that bringeth salvation hath appeared to all men, teaching us that, denying ungodliness and worldly lusts, we should live soberly, righteously, and godly, in this present world; looking for that blessed hope, and the glorious appearing of the great God and our Saviour Jesus Christ; who gave himself for us, that he might redeem us from all iniquity, and purify unto himself a peculiar people, zealous of good works" (Titus 2:11-14).

"Keep yourselves in the love of God, looking for the mercy of our Lord Jesus Christ unto eternal life. And of some have compassion, making a difference: and others save with fear, pulling them out of the fire; hating even the garment spotted by the flesh. Now unto him that is able to keep you from falling, and to present you faultless before the presence of his glory with exceeding joy, to the only wise God our Saviour, be glory and majesty, dominion and power, both now and ever" (Jude 1:21-25).

Getting to know King Jesus will bring you into a closer relationship with Him. It is what He desires the most, to be known by you. Reading His Word and meditating on it will show you God's heart and open yours to receive the knowledge and wisdom you need. You will also feel true love in a way you never felt before. God became a man, Jesus Christ, and sacrificed Himself for your sins. Surely there is no love that demonstrates greater than that!

"Nor height, nor depth, nor any other creature, shall be able to separate us from the love of God, which is in Christ Jesus our Lord" (Romans 8:39).

"Behold, what manner of love the Father hath bestowed upon us, that we should be called the sons of God: therefore the world knoweth us not, because it knew him not" (I John 3:1).

"Hereby perceive we the love of God, because he laid down his life for us: and we ought to lay down our lives for the brethren" (I John 3:16).

"And now abideth faith, hope, charity, these three; but the greatest of these is charity" (I Corinthians 13:13).

Knowing the King and having a relationship with Him is crucial to being a Palace Keeper. Think about the medieval days and how there was a huge castle to watch over. I'm sure there were only a few chosen men and women allowed to be near the king, and many were not allowed to have a real relationship with him. He had a big staff, and they each had a job. I bet you couldn't run to the king for every little thing. You had to know him and his ways.

Our King Jesus doesn't mind if you run to Him with every little thing. He is our Comforter and Tower of refuge in time of need. Knowing Jesus and who He really is will prepare your heart to serve Him better, even if you do have to run to Him every time you mess up.Having God's Word handy will help you when faced with problems. It is a manual filled with instructions on how to take care of impure feelings and thoughts. When some of the other tools seem to not be working, always lean on God's Word first. When you see anger and fear heading toward those tall iron gates, draw out His powerful sword of Scriptures and swing away!

"For the word of God is quick, and powerful, and sharper than any twoedged sword, piercing even to the dividing asunder of soul and spirit, and of the joints and marrow, and is a discerner of the thoughts and intents of the heart" (Hebrews 4:12).

God's Word has the message to purify our emotions! On the days when we don't feel like working to guard ourselves, Jesus gives us the motivation needed in the Scriptures. Here are examples of some emotions that will try to make their way into your heart. God's Word has instructions on how they can be defeated!

Anger

"Cease from anger, and forsake wrath: fret not thyself in any wise to do evil" (Psalm 37:8).

"A soft answer turneth away wrath: but grievous words stir up anger" (Proverbs 15:1).

"Let all bitterness, and wrath, and anger, and clamour, and evil speaking, be put away from you, with all malice: and be ye kind one to another, tenderhearted, forgiving one another, even as God for Christ's sake hath forgiven you" (Ephesians 4:31-32).

Fear

"In God I will praise his word, in God I have put my trust; I will not fear what flesh can do unto me" (Psalm 56:4).

"I called upon the LORD in distress: the LORD answered me, and set me in a large place. The LORD is on my side; I will not fear: what can man do unto me?" (Psalm 118:5-6).

"For God hath not given us the spirit of fear; but of power, and of love, and of a sound mind" (II Timothy 1:7).

Lust

"I am the LORD thy God, which brought thee out of the land of Egypt: open thy mouth wide, and I will fill it. But my people would not hearken to my voice; and Israel would none of me. So I gave them up unto their own hearts' lust: and they walked in their own counsels. Oh that my people had hearkened unto me, and Israel had walked in my ways!" (Psalm 81:10-13).

"For the commandment is a lamp; and the law is light; and reproofs of instruction are the way of life: to keep thee from the evil woman, from the flattery of the tongue of a strange woman. Lust not after her beauty in thine heart; neither let her take thee with her eyelids" (Proverbs 6:23-25).

"This I say then, Walk in the Spirit, and ye shall not fulfil the lust of the flesh. For the flesh lusteth against the Spirit, and the Spirit against the flesh: and these are contrary the one to the other: so that ye cannot do the things that ye would" (Galatians 5:16-17).

"For all that is in the world, the lust of the flesh, and the lust of the eyes, and the pride of life, is not of the Father, but is of the world. And the world passeth away, and the lust thereof: but he that doeth the will of God abideth for ever" (I John 2:16-17).

God's Word can defeat anything impure that comes your way. However, there is another tool that can help you organize those influences in your life.

Chapter 14: Tools of a Palace Keeper- Prayer

"Peace be within thy walls, and prosperity within thy palaces" (Psalm 122:7).

Having God's Word handy when you're faced with troubles goes hand and hand with this next tool: prayer. God's Word opens your mind to knowing King Jesus better, and prayer is a form of communication with Him. It doesn't just mean meditating on the Scriptures but includes speaking to the Lord one on one.

Prayer is known to unlock doors spiritually, allowing God's presence to flow like a fountain of refreshing water. Whether you know how to pray or not, prayer is a personal conversation with Jesus. When negative emotions try to pound at the front gates, and your mind is spinning on what to do, take a breather, be still, and pray. Asking God what He would like done in a situation blesses you with a new way of thinking. Instead of acting out of instinct or confused impulse, you will instead be calm and focused on handling the problem the right way, the way Jesus would handle them.

In a world that is spinning like an out-of-control merry-go-round, situations and decisions can seem like colorful blurs. Things are happening so fast, you don't seem to have much time to react at all, let alone the appropriate way. We almost feel like we need to make a decision as soon as possible; we feel rushed. We try to grab onto a solid pillar of stability for guidance, but we end up stumbling due to the momentum.

I am reminded of my niece. She loves to spin, especially if she has a cutesy, frilly dress on, which is almost every day. I even witnessed her napping in one of them! She does not want to take off her "princess dress." She loves to watch it float around her and play dance around the living room. She will spin, spin, and spin! Her giggles fill the air . . . until she has to stop. All of a sudden, her face is not so happy and she looks a little confused. It is almost like she forgot where she was or why everything is still a little blurry. My husband and I always chuckle because we know that as soon as the dizziness wears off, she will go off spinning again!

Life is like that. Trials, circumstances, and whatever else sends us spinning, spinning, and spinning until it's too much to handle. Prayer keeps us focused. It keeps our gaze on a solid pillar, much like a ballerina dancer. Have you ever wondered why ballerinas never seem to get dizzy, even after all those turns and fancy spins? They are taught to focus on a particular area of the room, preferably a corner. When they spin, their heads must snap toward that spot and their eyes must always land on it. The consistency of focusing on a still object enables them to stay on the right track.

Prayer must be our gaze landing on God, our solid pillar. He is our cornerstone of support and stability. When we turn, our focus should always snap in His direction. Here is what Psalm 66:20 says about God hearing our prayers:
"Blessed be God, which hath not turned away my prayer, nor his mercy from me."

He will never turn away your prayer! However, it may be answered in a totally different way than expected and in His time. Sometimes we can pray for things that may not be good for us, and if you find that a prayer has not been answered, it's probably in your best interest. Every word we speak to Jesus is heard. God has His hands on our hearts and understands the issues inside.

Pray to the Lord to have His way in your emotional and physical purity. Here is an example of what you could say:

Lord Jesus, thank You for this opportunity I have for growth and understanding. God, prepare my heart for what You have planned for my life. I pray that I can behave in the manner that pleases You, with all my mind, heart, body, and soul. Let Your will be done in me, and help me to trust what You are doing. Purify my emotions and replace any negative or evil intentions in my heart with Your positive and true love. In Jesus' name, Amen.

Prayer is effective when we truly acknowledge that the Bible is God's good and holy Word. We understand and know that the Scriptures are real and relevant to our lives today, just as they were relevant years ago. When we draw closer to Jesus, and His Word is being fed into our hearts, we are more open to hearing what He has to say.

"All scripture is given by inspiration of God, and is profitable for doctrine, for reproof, for correction, for instruction in righteousness" (II Timothy 3:16).

I was reading an online bible study by Bonnie Peacock on MoreToLifeToday.com, entitled "The Key to Answered Prayer." In it, she describes how without true understanding of who God really is, prayer will not mature the way it needs:

"Without a true understanding of God, we find ourselves treating Him like a genie, expecting Him to grant our every wish, or as a vending machine where we insert the correct change and make our selection. Neither of these approaches is effective."

But how do we pray if we never have prayed or have lost touch? Further in the Bible study, Bonnie wrote this quote that reached home for me.

"Prayer should not be the last resort but our first reaction."

The key to having solid prayer is not having any hesitation to seek God first.

"But without faith it is impossible to please him: for he that cometh to God must believe that he is, and that he is a rewarder of them that diligently seek him" (Hebrews 11:6).

I was always trying to depend on others to fill my expectations, and when they did not live up to them, it was like a brick in my heart. Every time I was disappointed with someone emotionally, on came another brick, then another after that, then one more after that. Soon, so much time had passed, I had lost track of how many bricks were laid. I was left with layers of resentment and pain. I had a wall of emotionally impure feelings. After time, I had even forgotten where the bricks came from! *Why did I get mad at him again? What did she say that got me feeling like I do? How come I can't get over this feeling of dislike toward them?*

Looking at the layered wall, it can be daunting. A feeling of being overwhelmed by the weight of emotional heaviness just sits, causing breath to run short of air. We can feel trapped and alone. I believe this is the reason why so many of us just keep ignoring the wall of emotional hurts, because it is too painful to return to it. The walls become our comfort, and we adapt by hiding behind them. *Are you ready for the good news?* Prayer can tear them down for you!

"The effectual fervent prayer of a righteous man availeth much" (James 5:16).

Imagine that every time you pray to God, a brick falls from that emotionally impure wall. The more you grow in the Lord and seek His face, the more bricks fall and the more His light shines through. When your walls of emotional expectations crumble, you will experience pure emotional freedom. God's light will be able to shine through you!

"He that hath no rule over his own spirit is like a city that is broken down, and without walls" (Proverbs 25:28).

When the bricks fall from our walls, God puts His own protection around us. It is not good to have your palace unprotected without a hedge of protection. As the Palace Keeper, making sure that you have the proper walls of protection is part of your job, but only the Lord Jesus Christ can provide such an excellent product!

"And the fortress of the high fort of thy walls shall he bring down, lay low, and bring to the ground, even to the dust. In that day shall this song be sung in the land of Judah; We have a strong city; salvation will God appoint for walls and bulwarks. Open ye the gates, that the righteous nation which keepeth the truth may enter in" (Isaiah 25:12-26:2).

One special ingredient to have effective and lively in your prayer is faith. You must believe that God can do great things in your life and the lives of others. It is not effective prayer to approach the throne of God *hoping* He will be sitting there. You must *know* that He will be sitting there, waiting for you. God doesn't need a set time to talk to you, but we need to give Him time to talk!

Prayer is not about a spiritual to-do list that you write and hand over to Jesus. It's not prescribing the medication to help out your problems and expecting the Great Physician to fix it your way. Prayer is not about self. It is about Him and making a connection with Him for His glory. When you admit to Him that the things in your life are not aligned right, you allow Him to align them for you.

Before the cleaning process can even begin, we must have the faith, or the knowledge, that God has what it takes to make us pure, inside and out. We all must believe that the King we serve can make something beautiful out of an unclean vessel. We must have faith that in God's power and authority, our best will be polished and our worst washed away. With God's Word, we will have knowledge. With prayer, we will be focused. And with faith, we will be prepared.

Chapter 15: Tools of a Palace Keeper- Faith

It was Peter's faith, Peter's knowledge of who God is, that allowed him to walk on the water with Jesus. How could Peter know if he stepped out of the boat that he would walk on water just like the Lord? He saw the opportunity to be faithful; the opportunity to exercise his knowledge. Peter seized the moment within the miracle and knew that if the Lord Jesus was there, he could get there.

We have heard this story many times, but *do we really understand faith? Do we really understand what it means to be faithful to God? Do we really know how much responsibility that holds?* To be faithful to God is to exercise our responsibility to obey what He says. His Word will be our fuel, and our communication by prayer will show us where we need to go. Our **faith** is the gas pedal, pushing forward down the path, while our unbelief is the brake pedal.

When we feel we have lost control of our circumstances and we feel that we have no grip on what is happening, we ease our foot on the brake pedal. Sometimes we panic and give it a good shove, causing others behind us to hesitate. We don't realize that we are being followed and that others watch our every move.

When we have a spout of unbelief and brake, we hinder others and cause the people behind us to brake in unbelief. It could be our closest friends or our younger siblings. They may see us living a holy life and be drawn to it. Without our knowledge, they are attached to us because they see the marvelous works of God in our life. Hopefully it is because they see Jesus's reflection in us.

Let's say you're cruising along the road of life. You make pit stops here and there, but that is not your final destination. On the road map, a red circle is around a place called heaven. You cannot wait to get there because you have heard so many great things about it! I mean, Jesus lives there! You go on, and colors pass you by. There may be a silence in the car for a while, and you suddenly start to feel lonely on this road trip. You started out rejoicing and singing, but now your foot is getting tired. I mean, you have been driving a really long time.

Suddenly you see a rest stop and your heart jumps. You get so excited until you look at the time. *Oh no,* you think. *If I stop now, I will never make it to heaven. If I take a break now, I won't make it! I have covered so much ground already, but my feet hurt and my back hurts. Oh, is that my stomach? Wow, I'm hungry!* You start debating back and forth whether to stop or keep going.

Your foot starts to ease on the brake, but your mind starts to spin more. If you stop now, you will never get to visit with Jesus, but if you don't, you will be so tired. As you debate, you don't even realize that the speedometer has lowered. You're like a snail slinking by. You are crawling and confused. In the midst of your confusion, you glance in your rearview mirror. *Oh no*, you think again. *There are so many other people behind me waiting for me to make a decision!*

Most of those following you will wait to see what you are going to do. However, some cannot wait on your time. Some are excited about visiting heaven, too, and they speed up and pass you by. As they pass, you can see them eating food and surrounded by things they packed for the trip. They were prepared before they even started the journey and have no need to stop. They have all that they need to get them to heaven. *Why did you not prepare?* I use this analogy to illustrate how we all are when it comes to our faith toward the purpose that God gives us. To get to heaven, we cannot have hesitation. In order to be a useful driver, we need to be an obedient and responsible one.

"Now faith is the substance of things hoped for, the evidence of things not seen. For by it the elders obtained a good report. Through faith we understand that the worlds were framed by the word of God, so that things which are seen were not made of things which do appear" (Hebrews 11:1-3).

"For whosoever shall call upon the name of the Lord shall be saved. How then shall they call on him in whom they have not believed? and how shall they believe in him of whom they have not heard? and how shall they hear without a preacher? And how shall they preach, except they be sent? as it is written, How beautiful are the feet of them that preach the gospel of peace, and bring glad tidings of good things! But they have not all obeyed the gospel. For Esaias saith, Lord, who hath believed our report? So then faith cometh by hearing, and hearing by the word of God" (Romans 10:13-17).

The part of the Scripture that stood out to me was the phrase, "But they have not all obeyed the gospel." Faith is the knowledge of who God is. When you know the Lord, you step on the gas pedal of faith. Galatians 5:5-6 brings us to the heart of faith. It speaks about the one thing that motivates the journey.

"For we through the Spirit wait for the hope of righteousness by faith. For in Jesus Christ neither circumcision availeth any thing, nor uncircumcision; but faith which worketh by love."

Love is the power behind everything Jesus does. It is the power that starts this journey to heaven, and love purifies the heart. Because of Christ's love for us and His demonstration of that love, we are forced to see how inadequate we really are compared to it.

Our faith, the gas pedal of our mobility, is powered by love. Love is the engine to your faith. Having a clean heart is not a onetime rest stop. To be pure the way the Lord instructs us to be takes a process. It takes a journey. We must remember where we are going on this road trip, and that is to heaven. We must first realize why we started the trip in the first place. Jesus wants us there with Him because He loves us! Hallelujah!

The road to purity is a narrow one. Only some of us will be willing and have enough faith to find it and go down it. Those of us who choose to continue in our impurity will be lost among the many faces that walk along the wide road.

"Enter ye in at the strait gate: for wide is the gate, and broad is the way, that leadeth to destruction, and many there be which go in thereat: because strait is the gate, and narrow is the way, which leadeth unto life, and few there be that find it" (Matthew 7:13-14).

When we see the line in the sand and have to make a decision as to whether we follow Jesus or not, it causes us to look at ourselves in an unflattering light. A Palace Keeper will never progress if he/she never look at what they are doing wrong and take the steps to make it right. Faith is an incredible tool, but once we use it, we are forced to see how sinful we are in comparison to God. This leads to the next and probably the hardest tool to implement: repentance.

Chapter 16: Tools of a Palace Keeper- Repentance

"Therefore say unto the house of Israel, Thus saith the Lord GOD; Repent, and turn yourselves from your idols; and turn away your faces from all your abominations" **(Ezekiel 14:6).**

It is true that when we see how unclean our hearts really are, it doesn't feel good. No one likes that feeling of being dirty. Yet we must approach a situation honestly, noticing that it was because of our weakness that we are unclean, not because God can't do anything about it. God isn't standing by with a dish towel and deciding we are not worth being wiped clean!

"Woe unto you, scribes and Pharisees, hypocrites! for ye make clean the outside of the cup and of the platter, but within they are full of extortion and excess. Thou blind Pharisee, cleanse first that which is within the cup and platter, that the outside of them may be clean also. Woe unto you, scribes and Pharisees, hypocrites! for ye are like unto whited sepulchres, which indeed appear beautiful outward, but are within full of dead men's bones, and of all uncleanness" (Matthew 23:25-27)

If we think Jesus is just standing far away with a towel and is choosing not to clean our uncleanness, we have not read the Scripture properly.

Being a Palace Keeper is to believe that God can complete a transformation from wickedness to righteousness. **Repentance** is not a form of criticism from God. It is not a negative force to throw your mistakes back at you. It is a positive tool in which the Lord allows us to fully commit to Him as we make the decision to turn away from those bad influences with godly fear.

"Favor is deceitful, and beauty is vain: but a woman that feareth the LORD, she shall be praised" (Proverbs 31:30).

Godly fear does not mean what we think it means. It does not mean to be scared of God but it means to be fearful of displeasing Him. To have the "fear of the Lord" is to have the desire to follow in the Lord's way. Proverbs 31:30 speaks of a woman who is not afraid of a wrathful, hateful God because that is not how our God is. It speaks about a woman who is God fearing, a heart that wants to please the Lord and not go against His ways. Without that godly fear, we disregard God's instructions. Godly fear is a reverence and an acknowledgement of the His sovereignty. When we have a God-fearing heart and desire for purity, Proverbs 31:30 says that should be praised!

"In those days came John the Baptist, preaching in the wilderness of Judaea, and saying, Repent ye: for the kingdom of heaven is at hand. For this is he that was spoken of by the prophet Esaias, saying, The voice of one crying in the wilderness, Prepare ye the way of the Lord, make his paths straight" (Matthew 3:1-3).
"Now after that John was put in prison, Jesus came into Galilee, preaching the gospel of the kingdom of God, and saying, The time is fulfilled, and the kingdom of God is at hand: repent ye, and believe the gospel" (Mark 1:14-15).

Here are some definitions of the word "repent":

1. To feel remorse, contrition, or self-reproach for what one has done or failed to do; *be contrite.*

2. To feel such regret for past conduct as to change one's mind regarding it: repented of intemperate behavior.

3. To make a change for the better as a result of remorse or contrition for one's sins.

I find it interesting and fitting how these definitions are laid out. When we are made aware of our sinful nature and reminded of our sins which have displeased God, our first reaction is to feel sad and remorseful.

Being a Palace Keeper doesn't mean we will be a perfect worker. It means that we are working toward perfection in Christ. We will make mistakes even through the cleansing process. The important part is not trying to eliminate mistakes entirely by our own effort, which is impossible, but to turn from doing the same mistakes again and again.

"Enter not into the path of the wicked, and go not in the way of evil men. Avoid it, pass not by it, turn from it, and pass away" (Proverbs 4:14-15).

"This know also, that in the last days perilous times shall come. For men shall be lovers of their own selves, covetous, boasters, proud, blasphemers, disobedient to parents, unthankful, unholy, without natural affection, trucebreakers, false accusers, incontinent, fierce, despisers of those that are good, traitors, heady, highminded, lovers of pleasures more than lovers of God; having a form of godliness, but denying the power thereof: from such turn away" (II Timothy 3:1-5).

When the passage in II Timothy started listing the sins we are all guilty of, I began to get a little sensitive about it until I read the last part: "from such turn away." God wants us to understand and recognize what is unclean and unacceptable behavior in His eyes. Repentance is recognizing the sins of your past and present and making the decision to turn from them.

"Ye shall walk after the LORD your God, and fear him, and keep his commandments, and obey his voice, and ye shall serve him, and cleave unto him" (Deuteronomy 13:4).

"The LORD is nigh unto them that are of a broken heart; and saveth such as be of a contrite spirit" (Psalm 34:18).

In one of the definitions for repentance, it mentioned "to be contrite." The Lord is near to those who have a broken heart and a contrite spirit. Jesus wants us to be healed and purified. The encounter we have with Him as our hearts become broken because we see our impurity is a divine one. To be a broken vessel at the feet of the King, admitting that you've done wrong, is an important part of repentance. The other is acknowledging that you need to change and turn from what you've done.

To be contrite is the desire for atonement. In our spirit, in order to achieve true repentance, we must have the desire to reconcile with God. Once we have reconciled and have allowed God to change our hearts, we must make the decision never to go back to the sin we had committed.

"Thy mercy, O LORD, is in the heavens; and thy faithfulness reacheth unto the clouds" (Psalm 36:5).

Maybe we can understand repentance more if we read some verses of Scripture that talk about God's mercy and forgiveness. Most of us think we have sinned and messed up so bad that the situation cannot be fixed. Maybe we feel that we have gone so far from His hands that we are not within His grasp any more. However, God loves you too much not to have something in place to help save you. The Lord's mercy is good and endures forever!

"O give thanks unto the LORD; for he is good: for his mercy endureth for ever" (Psalm 118:29).

"All the paths of the LORD are mercy and truth unto such as keep his covenant and his testimonies" (Psalm 25:10).

"For thou, Lord, art good, and ready to forgive; and plenteous in mercy unto all them that call upon thee" (Psalm 86:5).

Jesus is ready to forgive! His mercy is never failing and is always flowing. Call upon Him when you are broken in your heart, when you are weary of your crying, and when deep in your soul you want to make things right with your King!

"If thou, LORD, shouldest mark iniquities, O Lord, who shall stand? But there is forgiveness with thee, that thou mayest be feared. I wait for the LORD, my soul doth wait, and in his word do I hope" (Psalm 130:3-5).

"To open their eyes, and to turn them from darkness to light, and from the power of Satan unto God, that they may receive forgiveness of sins, and inheritance among them which are sanctified by faith that is in me" (Acts 26:18).

"To the praise of the glory of his grace, wherein he hath made us accepted in the beloved. In whom we have redemption through his blood, the forgiveness of sins, according to the riches of his grace" (Ephesians 1:6-7).

To have a change occur in your heart is to have applied true repentance. This change needs to be effected by our Provider and not forced by our human instincts to fix things. Jesus loves you and is here to help you reach your full potential. When you are on the job, Palace Keeper, and you stumble and fall, turn toward the One who will lift you. God is the Provider of change but He Himself does not change. So, if you find yourself scrambling to get up after losing your balance, look up, and He will be there!

"For I am the LORD, I change not; therefore ye sons of Jacob are not consumed. Even from the days of your fathers ye are gone away from mine ordinances, and have not kept them. Return unto me, and I will return unto you, saith the LORD of hosts" (Malachi 3:6-7).

"Now there are diversities of gifts, but the same Spirit. And there are differences of administrations, but the same Lord. And there are diversities of operations, but it is the same God which worketh all in all" (I Corinthians 12:4-6).

Remember when we talked about one of God's tools called faith? It wasn't that long ago! We have to remind ourselves each day that when we fall, we don't have to stay down. As God has revealed to us who He is through His Word and prayer, we can have faith to trust Him and can dust ourselves off to move forward. Once we make a decision in our hearts to turn from our sin, we have just uncovered another tool of a Palace Keeper.

Chapter 17: Tools of a Palace Keeper-
Baptism

**"Then Peter said unto them, Repent, and
be baptized every one of you in the name of
Jesus Christ for the remission of sins, and
ye shall receive the gift of the Holy Ghost"
(Acts 2:38).**

As we walk through our daily lives, it is very
easy to stumble. Many times, we are just not
looking at where our feet are going but are
following the many voices that call our names.
Purity needs to be more than a thought, more
than an idea. It needs to be an active
commitment inside you and made manifest in
your lifestyle. To be pure is to be clean. Usually,
when something is dirty, what do we use to
clean it? Water!

The Bible compares water to the blood of
Jesus. *Ew, how can someone be clean if they
are washed in blood?* Spiritually, we can!
Physically, not so much. . . .

Isaiah 1:16-17 says **"Wash you, make you
clean; put away the evil of your doings from
before mine eyes; cease to do evil; learn to
do well; seek judgment, relieve the
oppressed, judge the fatherless, plead for
the widow."**

We are commanded to be washed, *but why?* In the Old Testament, God established specific things that people had to do in order to have their sins washed clean. The main way was to sacrifice a pure animal. Not just any ol' animal; God had specifications for that, too.

However, it didn't take long for the people to start abusing God's system. It's not because the system had flaws; after all, it was created by the Almighty. It was because the people, human beings, were flawed and manipulated the system. The entire purpose was for the purity of God's people, to perfect them and to draw them closer to Him. Instead, the people just kept sinning and sacrificing and did not turn altogether from their sin. There was no true repentance. They would make the choice every day to sin and made the sacrificing a routine.

That is not what the Lord wanted. He loves us and does not want us to fall. God wants a relationship and not a religion. Man had turned the system that God created in love into a tradition, and their hearts remained unclean. In the New Testament, our great big God, the Master of the universe, did something spectacular; He humbled Himself and took the form of the sacrifice. What a great expression of His love for us! It was like God said, "I know what you need, and I'm going to be that for you."

If the old covenant required a pure sacrifice, this covenant also required one, but it needed to be purer than the other sacrifice in order for it to accomplish its purpose. How can you get a purer sacrifice than an innocent lamb? Jesus, our sinless Father, became that lamb to save us; that's how!

"The next day John seeth Jesus coming unto him, and saith, Behold the Lamb of God, which taketh away the sin of the world" (John 1:29).
"And if ye call on the Father, who without respect of persons judgeth according to every man's work, pass the time of your sojourning here in fear: forasmuch as ye know that ye were not redeemed with corruptible things, as silver and gold, from your vain conversation received by tradition from your fathers; but with the precious blood of Christ, as of a lamb without blemish and without spot: who verily was foreordained before the foundation of the world, but was manifest in these last times for you, who by him do believe in God, that raised him up from the dead, and gave him glory; that your faith and hope might be in God" (I Peter 1:17-21).

God became that living sacrifice so that we may be cleansed by His blood! When Jesus walked this earth, He preached and was preparing His children for this new cleansing process. His desire was and is for our hearts to be washed, to be made clean, just as white as snow!

"Come now, and let us reason together, saith the LORD: though your sins be as scarlet, they shall be as white as snow; though they be red like crimson, they shall be as wool" (Isaiah 1:18).

Baptism is the obedience to cleanliness, where a person must be fully immersed in water. The word "baptism" in green means "baptizo" or fully wet. When someone comes out of the water during baptism, the Word tells us they become a new person!
"Therefore we are buried with him by baptism into death: that like as Christ was raised up from the dead by the glory of the Father, even so we also should walk in newness of life. For if we have been planted together in the likeness of his death, we shall be also in the likeness of his resurrection: knowing this, that our old man is crucified with him, that the body of sin might be destroyed, that henceforth we should not serve sin" (Romans 6:4-6.)

Baptism is a spiritual burial of our old sinful self. It connects us with the sacrifice that Jesus made with His own life on the cross. We spiritually cover ourselves with that sacrifice, which has power to cleanse us of sin. Palace Keeper, as you are on the job, you will get to the place where you have used great tools to keep the palace pure. However, if you have not initiated the power of baptism, your heart will never be fully clean. A heart that is pumped by blood needs to be covered by His blood! Our old hearts need to be washed by the sacrifice of Jesus so that we are able to receive a new one!

"Create in me a clean heart, O God; and renew a right spirit within me" (Psalm 51:10).

King Jesus wants to see all of us with a new heart! He says so right in His Word; we need to all be baptized and receive His Spirit in order to make it to heaven.

"Jesus answered, Verily, verily, I say unto thee, Except a man be born of water and of the Spirit, he cannot enter into the kingdom of God" (John 3:5).

If we are baptized and come out of the water a new person, that means we are reborn in Christ. Day by day, we face temptations sore. We all make mistakes and fall short. Palace Keeper, if you use the tools we talked about so far *except* for this one, you will soon find that something is missing. You will still feel incomplete and filthy. Even if you read God's Word and know that Jesus is God. Even if you develop a relationship, pray, and have true knowledge. Even with faith and deep repentance. If we are not baptized in Jesus' name, our hearts will stay in an impure state. *How can we be washed clean if we don't get wet?*

Purifying your heart takes more than just a sprinkle. Remember when you would play outside as a kid, and you came in all muddy and gross? Mom wasn't too happy. Yet, she didn't just say "Oh, just put your hand in the water and splash some drops on your face." Uh, yeah right! She said, "You are so dirty! Go in the bathroom and take a shower!" Mom knew that just a handful of water droplets were not going to be effective. You had to get *under* the water to get clean!

That is what baptism is: getting under the water, in the precious name of Jesus, and cleansing your heart of all the yucky stuff that has been built up. It's not enough to just sit by the bathtub, praying that the water will magically jump out and wash you. No! Once you use the tools of God (the Word, prayer, faith, repentance), you are already prepared to stop hoverin' and start dunkin'! Take that step into the water and make that commitment to purity. Make sure it's sealed by the name of Jesus. After all, His blood is what made this possible.

"Then said Paul, John verily baptized with the baptism of repentance, saying unto the people, that they should believe on him which should come after him, that is, on Christ Jesus. When they heard *this,* they were baptized in the name of the Lord Jesus." (Acts 19:4-5).

"For as many of you as have been baptized into Christ have put on Christ" (Galatians 3:27).

God's plan for your life is much bigger than you know. Purity helps us stay in tune with what God wants to do and draws us closer to Him. Understanding that we need to be washed is acknowledging that Jesus did not sacrifice Himself without a purpose.

"If we say that we have fellowship with him, and walk in darkness, we lie, and do not the truth: but if we walk in the light, as he is in the light, we have fellowship one with another, and the blood of Jesus Christ his Son cleanseth us from all sin. If we say that we have no sin, we deceive ourselves, and the truth is not in us. If we confess our sins, he is faithful and just to forgive us our sins, and to cleanse us from all unrighteousness. If we say that we have not sinned, we make him a liar, and his word is not in us" (I John 1:6-10).

He didn't die for nothing! Jesus Christ died to cleanse you and me from sin. If we choose as Palace Keepers to ignore the tool that is baptism, what we do when we are on the job really won't matter. It's like knowing there's a mop nearby and you just stare at all the dirty footprints in the hallway. *How can we protect ourselves from being impure and not take the step to wash away our past impurities?* God doesn't want us to hold onto the dirt. God wants to get rid of it! He doesn't want you to live in filth. He wants your palace to be the cleanest place ever!

Along with baptism, Jesus provides a gift. This gift is actually the next tool that God has for us Palace Keepers to use to keep our palaces pure.

Chapter 18: Tools of a Palace Keeper- Holy Ghost

As I'm writing this chapter, I can look outside to the beautiful New England foliage. It takes my breath away not just because it's lovely, but also because I can feel the wind blowing through my window. Though I cannot see the wind, I still know it's there. I don't just hear it in the auburn, orange-colored trees; I feel it in my bones.

The Word of God compares the **Holy Ghost** or the Holy Spirit to the wind. It's something we cannot see but is something we can feel. We may not know where it's going, but we know what it touches. How? We can see what it affects.

"Jesus answered, Verily, verily, I say unto thee, Except a man be born of water and of the Spirit, he cannot enter into the kingdom of God. That which is born of the flesh is flesh; and that which is born of the Spirit is spirit. Marvel not that I said unto thee, Ye must be born again.The wind bloweth where it listeth, and thou hearest the sound thereof, but canst not tell whence it cometh, and whither it goeth: so is every one that is born of the Spirit" (John 3:5-8).

The Holy Ghost is God's Spirit. The wonderful thing is Jesus wants His Spirit living inside you! We are made in His image, yet Jesus wants to be so much closer to us than that. The Lord wants to be right where He knows your treasure is; in your heart!

"For where your treasure is, there will your heart be also" (Matthew 6:21).

Purity of the heart can be guided down a much straighter path when you have God's Spirit driving it. This is the greatest gift anyone can ever receive, our glorious King Jesus living in our palace! We have talked about the different parts of the palace and how the King needs to be in the throne room. Before the King can even sit on that throne, He needs to be invited into the palace. *If He is not even in the building, how can He sit in a chamber?* As the Palace Keeper, it's your job to open the doors to let Jesus in. You must receive the King and allow Him to reign. Jesus says in the Bible that His Spirit is available for everyone to receive. Every living person is a walking palace, in need of King Jesus to enter and to dwell. The Lord has promised that if He is received, He will comfort us and not leave us!

"And it shall come to pass in the last days, saith God, I will pour out of my Spirit upon all flesh: and your sons and your daughters shall prophesy, and your young men shall see visions, and your old men shall dream dreams" (Acts 2:17).

"I will not leave you comfortless: I will come to you" (John 14:18).

"Let your conversation be without covetousness; and be content with such things as ye have: for he hath said, I will never leave thee, nor forsake thee" (Hebrews 13:5).

On the Day of Pentecost, people were waiting in the upper room for the promise that Jesus said He would send. They didn't know what to expect, but they knew they needed to receive it. As they waited, they didn't just sit around. They prayed together and were unified. They put their focus on God. Then an amazing thing happened. The Lord's Spirit filled the entire place and everyone there! The promise had finally arrived!

"And when the day of Pentecost was fully come, they were all with one accord in one place. And suddenly there came a sound from heaven as of a rushing mighty wind, and it filled all the house where they were sitting. And there appeared unto them cloven tongues like as of fire, and it sat upon each of them. And they were all filled with the Holy Ghost, and began to speak with other tongues, as the Spirit gave them utterance" (Acts 2:1-4).

As the Holy Ghost filled the people, they began to speak in other languages. The Scripture says that the Spirit "came [as] a sound from heaven" *and* "as of a rushing mighty wind." Have you walked around downtown in a city before? When the wind blows, you can hear it in between the buildings. That's what receiving the Holy Ghost is like. There is sound when the Spirit begins to live in someone's heart. To be fair to God, we cannot assume that He only knows one language. Jesus is the Lord of all creation and of all the nations! He is not just the God of America but He's also the God of the whole world! Receiving the Holy Spirit is more than speaking in other languages; that is the evidence that Jesus has come to live in us.

Palace Keeper, when you open that door for the King of kings to enter, what do you hear? Of course, there has to be some sort of fanfare sound, like a trumpet or a horn. *When royalty arrives at a palace, isn't there always someone there making an announcement by sound?* When you receive God's Spirit into your heart, you become that instrument in announcing that King Jesus is here! Having the Holy Ghost is having Jesus in your palace. It is the perfect way to make sure your heart is moving in the right direction. Who better to guide you to true purity than the purest of them all?

The Holy Spirit is one of God's tools because it's a personal and intimate way for Him to be in the place He cares about most. Baptism washes you, but the Holy Ghost keeps you. It will be the Voice when there are many other voices trying to get your attention. The wonderful thing is once you have this tool to use, it never goes away! The Holy Ghost is forever dwelling in your heart. When you have Jesus living inside you, you will be able to use these next tools better.

Chapter 19: Tools of a Palace Keeper- Obedience

The topic of obedience is one that can be the most sensitive to discuss because it deals with someone's personal commitment. It is too easy to feel inadequate and yet prideful at the same time when we think about the different things we must obey in our lives. We know that deep down we can make a deeper commitment but in reality we have not. So when we see an example of someone being more obedient than we are, we take it as a threat instead of accepting them as an example and learning from them.

Like I said before, we can get a little sensitive. So when we think about **obedience** and what it means, we have to humble ourselves. The primary purpose is to glorify Jesus with our entire heart, mind, body, and soul.

"Who can say, I have made my heart clean, I am pure from my sin? Divers weights, and divers measures, both of them are alike abomination to the LORD. Even a child is known by his doings, whether his work be pure, and whether it be right" (Proverbs 20:9-11).

Purity should be worn like a garment, wrapped around us like a robe of protection. It should be treated like a high-end jacket. I remember walking into an expensive department store in search of a nice coat. I knew the style I needed, but most importantly, I knew my price range.

I actually had walked into the pricey store, hoping to score some deals off a clearance rack. I don't consider myself cheap, but I do feel that it is silly to pay full price for something if you know you can get it on sale.

As I walked down the aisle, I saw them, the most beautiful jackets I had ever seen! They had bold patterns yet were classic designs, almost out of the closet of a 1950s movie star. Some were simple in color but perfect in cut. I tried one on and was in awe of how it fit. It was like the jacket was made especially for me! After some high-pitched shrieks within myself (though I am sure some of it squeaked out as I noticed my husband glanced at me from a couple of racks away), I eagerly looked at the price tag. Two hundred dollars! For a piece of clothing? Don't get me wrong, I can buy clothes for two hundred dollars, but I will have many different pieces of clothing to make numerous outfits, not just *one* piece of clothing.

Slightly disappointed and somewhat enraged, I put it back on the rack. My curiosity got to me, so I glanced at the *"instructions for care"* tag on the neck. How many of us have made a decision about what to buy based on the upkeep it needs? I have too many times. We are just too busy to care about one piece in our entire wardrobe. When I looked at the tag, I thought, *Oh, it's dry-clean only. That is too much work!* I left the store feeling disgusted and continued my search for a jacket that was less expensive and didn't need much upkeep.

Isn't that how we are with the garment of purity that God provides? We search for something to protect us, to cover us, and we walk into His throne room. The Lord hands over the garment of purity, and it looks magnificent. It is white as snow and without spot or blemish, the highest quality anyone could ever produce. We look at the tag on the neck and it reads, "God-cleaned only." That sounds simple enough to take care of. I mean, He cleans it for us and we don't have to do too much to keep it that way, right? So we eagerly try it on and wow! How wonderful it fits and looks! We feel amazing in it and enjoy it for that moment. However, our eyes wander around the garment and we spot a price tag tangling from one of the arms. It reads, **"Full obedience to God."**

What? Oh, no, we think, I can't do that! I don't have time to devote to God that way to dedicate to wearing this garment all the time. I have school, work, friends, and a job at the church. My schedule is full already. I have too much going on for this. My life is just too busy to pay this price. It is too expensive! So we take it off, hand it back to God, and walk away frustrated and upset. We leave in search of a less expensive price tag.

Purity, full and entirely clean purity, will only happen with a willing heart that will dedicate its full obedience to the Lord Jesus Christ. We cannot clean the garment of purity on our own with our own supplies. We don't know how to properly handle it. It must be "God-cleaned only."

To put on the garment of purity is not just to protect your body but also the heart that lies inside. It is not just a physical protection but an emotional protection as well. It can protect and cleanse bad attitudes, unholy motivations, grudges, bitterness, selfishness, lies, self-righteousness, and rebellion. The garment is spotless and white, as long as we give our utmost obedience to God to maintain it. Once we shy away from that, the garment will get dirty, and we make a terrible mess trying to clean it ourselves.

"Keep yourselves in the love of God, looking for the mercy of our Lord Jesus Christ unto eternal life. And of some have compassion, making a difference: and others save with fear, pulling them out of the fire; hating even the garment spotted by the flesh" (Jude 1:21-23).

I used to have this gorgeous dressy top. Did you catch that? I said "used to." The tag on the neck read "dry-clean only," but I totally disregarded the instruction when I dropped some spaghetti sauce on it. Isn't that always the case with spaghetti?

My mother-in-law and I laugh about this all the time because it never fails to happen when we wear white; we always end up eating something with sauce! No matter how careful we are, we end up wearing it. Out of all the sauces, spaghetti sauce is like a food bomb on clothes. Once it drops, it splatters, and destruction is everywhere!

So instead of taking my time to clean it right, I rushed the job and acted on impulse. I grabbed a rag, ran it under hot water and rubbed the stain right in. Not on purpose but my disobedience to the directions created a huge spot on my pretty top. Even worse, I threw it into the wash and made that stain permanent. What a dope I was! The shirt didn't even look anywhere near clean. It didn't even look like I tried. It looked even worse than a spaghetti stain! It was a pitiful result from my pitiful attempt.

"Therefore also now, saith the LORD, turn ye even to me with all your heart, and with fasting, and with weeping, and with mourning: and rend your heart, and not your garments, and turn unto the LORD your God: for he is gracious and merciful, slow to anger, and of great kindness, and repenteth him of the evil" (Joel 2:12-13).

When God instructs us that the garment of purity is "God-clean only", why do we try to clean it ourselves in our own pitiful attempts? Do we feel like God ran out of supplies to clean it properly? Are we trying to do Him a favor? We need to give full obedience and not semi-obedience when it feels convenient for us. "Full" means "all." Total dependence on Jesus leads to total purity and cleanliness.

Purity is not just about our human relationships. It is about a cleansing process between the Creator and the creation, which involves clearing away anything that will hinder the creation from having a fulfilling relationship with its Creator. I am noticing more than ever that when I put on the Lord's purity garment, I nonverbally told Him that I was applying His cleansing principles to my entire person. Not just to my flesh but to every single part of myself. The key is to never take it off.

"Awake, awake; put on thy strength, O Zion; put on thy beautiful garments, O Jerusalem, the holy city: for henceforth there shall no more come into thee the uncircumcised and the unclean. Shake thyself from the dust; arise, and sit down, O Jerusalem: loose thyself from the bands of thy neck, O captive daughter of Zion. For thus saith the LORD, Ye have sold yourselves for nought; and ye shall be redeemed without money" (Isaiah 52:1-3).

"Thou hast a few names even in Sardis which have not defiled their garments; and they shall walk with me in white: for they are worthy. He that overcometh, the same shall be clothed in white raiment; and I will not blot out his name out of the book of life, but I will confess his name before my Father, and before his angels" (Revelation 3:4-5).

To coincide with putting on the garment of purity, we also have to be obedient in taking off the garment of the flesh. All filthiness and uncleanliness that is wrapped around us, Jesus wants us to shed and replace with His cleanliness and godliness. When we have something that is unclean in our hearts, our obedience to the Lord and His instruction will help us to get rid of anything impure. We have the ability as a Palace Keeper through obedience to throw any bad influences from our palace.

Obedience to the Lord's instructions can purge impurity. The word "purge" has a couple of different meanings, but they all lead to the same result; that is, to be clean.

Purge: a: to clear of guilt b: to free from moral or ceremonial defilement/ to make free of something unwanted

Let's not forget that you are a Palace Keeper now. You have a job assigned to you, and God has provided you with many tools and resources to accomplish this job the right way. Jesus is reaching out with an opportunity to obey, and when you yield and grab on, He will lift you from the darkness and into His cleansing light!

In the Book of Acts, Peter and some other apostles obeyed the Word of the Lord by preaching what Jesus taught them. They yielded to the Lord and healed the sick. Their obedience to God did not come without a price. They were thrown into prison because of it.

"Then the high priest rose up, and all they that were with him, (which is the sect of the Sadducees,) and were filled with indignation, and laid their hands on the apostles, and put them in the common prison" (Acts 5:17-18).

End of story, right? Not with God! Peter and the apostles were not even in prison a full day before help came. Their obedience to God's instruction found favor in His sight, and they were able to continue being useful vessels for His kingdom.

"But the angel of the Lord by night opened the prison doors, and brought them forth, and said, Go, stand and speak in the temple to the people all the words of this life. And when they heard that, they entered into the temple early in the morning, and taught. But the high priest came, and they that were with him, and called the council together, and all the senate of the children of Israel, and sent to the prison to have them brought. But when the officers came, and found them not in the prison, they returned, and told, saying, The prison truly found we shut with all safety, and the keepers standing without before the doors: but when we had opened, we found no man within. Now when the high priest and the captain of the temple and the chief priests heard these things, they doubted of them whereunto this would grow. Then came one and told them, saying, Behold, the men whom ye put in prison are standing in the temple, and teaching the people" (Acts 5:19-25).

When Peter and the apostles were thrown into prison, do you think they sat there and pouted? Do you think they doubted Jesus and His purpose for them? In their hearts, they had the knowledge of Him that allowed them to obey without complaint or lack of faith. When they were brought forward to the council, Peter expressed a boldness as he addressed the officer's and the high priest's accusations.

"And when they had brought them, they set them before the council: and the high priest asked them, saying, Did not we straitly command you that ye should not teach in this name? and, behold, ye have filled Jerusalem with your doctrine, and intend to bring this man's blood upon us. Then Peter and the other apostles answered and said, We ought to obey God rather than men. The God of our fathers raised up Jesus, whom ye slew and hanged on a tree. Him hath God exalted with his right hand to be a Prince and a Saviour, for to give repentance to Israel, and forgiveness of sins. And we are his witnesses of these things; and so is also the Holy Ghost, whom God hath given to them that obey him" (Acts 5:27-32).

Wow, it doesn't sound like someone who has suffered behind bars! When our backs are against the wall and we feel like what we stand for is in jeopardy, what will we do? Will we stand for our beliefs and responsibility as a Palace Keeper? Are we ready, when we obey God, to acknowledge that the world might be against us?

There will be some people who will see your Christ-like example as refreshing, in a world that is emotionally promiscuous. Yet there will be others who will mock and feel threatened by your choice to remain pure. Why they feel that way is not your problem. Yet how you react to those situations when they arise will reflect on the God you serve. Obeying Him will give you the protection you need when under the attacks of the unrighteous. There is an end to this example, but I urge you to read it for yourself. Peter's words were not heard with willing hearts, and he and the rest of the apostles with him were beaten. Yet they rejoiced for being worthy enough to suffer for Christ's sake.

Prepare your heart from those who may not understand what the gospel says about purity. True obedience is an act within you. It means to take action when something has been revealed to you. It's not a quick and impulsive action but one backed with knowledge and wisdom from our King Jesus. Obedience is a big part of this entire cleansing process. If we do not obey how to be clean, are we ever going to be clean?

Being baptized in Jesus' name and receiving the gift of the Holy Ghost according to the Scripture is a vital part of the cleansing process as well. This is being obedient to God's Word and is necessary in having a true relationship with the King. After all, Jesus is the King of kings and Lord of lords. He has all the knowledge and power to make an unclean vessel spotless. In your obedience and your willingness to obey the true purity, it can be made manifest within you.

Chapter 20: Tools of a Palace Keeper- Discernment

"And they shall teach my people the difference between the holy and profane, and cause them to discern between the unclean and the clean" (Ezekiel 44:23).

"Then shall ye return, and discern between the righteous and the wicked, between him that serveth God and him that serveth him not" (Malachi 3:18).

The definition of insanity is doing the same thing over and over again, expecting a different result. If that's the case, then lock us all up please, because we are all guilty! *Why do we do the same thing a second time, when we know it didn't work the first time?* That is human nature. There is a natural order in the way things work. Part of that is we are always falling back to being ignorant and disobedient as creation. Not as a child of God should be, we fall back to that irresponsible, selfish, emotionally impure state. If God sees that in your heart you are willing to do what it takes to change your promiscuous motives, He will change your motives to purity in time. We cannot change them on our own. We can "reform" them, meaning changing our habits to correct ones; those only change on the surface. God is the only One who can bring up those roots of impurity and replant. So when will we hand over the shovel? Here are some definitions of **discernment**:

1. the quality of being able to grasp and comprehend what is obscure: skill in discerning
2. an act of perceiving

God has given us the tool of discernment to help us perceive and grasp bad from good. Instead of doing the same sin over and over, if we apply the right principle of discernment to our lives, our perception will be transformed. When I was dating my husband, I was obsessive and needy, the total opposite of my true self. *How did that happen? How did I allow myself to be a slave to my own emotions?*

Looking back, I had not used the tool of discernment. My husband was in the throne room, where God should have been. It took a few years for that to change correctly. Yes, I tried to "reform" my habits, and that worked for a while. Yet my intentions and motives did not change, and I was still allowing God to come second in my relationships. I didn't have God as the King of my Palace, reigning where He belongs. He was wandering around the hallways somewhere!

Finally, I began to understand more about what discernment meant and that it required some real action on my part. Things then began to turn around not by my own positioning, but by the hand of God. I had reached a point where God was on my back burner, waiting patiently. It wasn't that my husband was perfect like the Lord, but my emotions were boiling over so much that he became perfect in my own eyes. Remember idolatry and the golden calf that Aaron made? I also thought I was perfect in the role of a female Christian.

God started working, and when He starts working on us, our world can shift in a quick moment. He showed me that just because I looked like a Christian, my heart was not in God's favor. My emotions were not Christ-like. Actually, they were anything but pure. They were all over the place! I had no emotional discernment.

Many of us are falling victim to this situation every day. It's come to a point where even some girls and boys in our churches are allowing bad influences into their palaces because they have not practiced proper discernment. Stand strong and realize that the Lord is your only Provider for true happiness and true purity. Discerning what is right and wrong for your heart will bring you far more than you could ever imagine. For a lot of people, my husband and I included, it wasn't that we chose to be emotionally impure. We had not properly guarded our hearts, and we became so engulfed in one another that it became easier for danger to not just lurk but to happen. We were too busy looking at each other instead of standing together, looking in the same direction.

"Get wisdom, get understanding: forget it not; neither decline from the words of my mouth. Forsake her not, and she shall preserve thee: love her, and she shall keep thee. Wisdom is the principal thing; therefore get wisdom: and with all thy getting get understanding" (Proverbs 4:5-7).

"And give unto Solomon my son a perfect heart, to keep thy commandments, thy testimonies, and thy statutes, and to do all these things, and to build the palace, for the which I have made provision" (I Chronicles 29:19).

In I Kings 3, we read that king Solomon created a relationship with the pharaoh of Egypt and made Pharaoh's daughter his wife. Solomon brought his wife into the city of David, where the people were worshiping idols. The Scripture records that Solomon loved the Lord; however, he still sacrificed to these false gods. Solomon sinned greatly, and though he apparently loved the Lord, his actions did not glorify God at all. In I Kings 3:4, Solomon went to Gibeon and burnt a thousand offerings upon the altar for God. This action brought about a miraculous thing: Jesus appeared to Solomon in a dream!

"In Gibeon the Lord appeared to Solomon in a dream by night: and God said, Ask what I shall give thee" (I Kings 3:5).

Wow, can you believe that? Though Solomon was a great sinner, God still wanted to bless him. He gave Solomon a chance to ask for anything and God would give it to him. Oh my, if the Lord had appeared unto us with the same question, what would we ask for? I believe we would have materialistic things in mind at first, until maybe those filtered to the back of the line. So what did Solomon ask?

"Give therefore thy servant an understanding heart to judge thy people, that I may discern between good and bad: for who is able to judge this thy so great a people?" (I Kings 3:9).

Solomon recognized that his heart was wicked and he needed discernment. He realized that his past decisions were not right, and he wanted to make himself right with the Lord. Solomon asked for an understanding heart and for wisdom, that he may be able to discern between the good and the bad. *Now really, would you and I ask for that?* I am not sure, but Solomon did. In verse 10 we can read God's reaction.

"And the speech pleased the Lord, that Solomon had asked this thing" (I Kings 3:10).

When we are on the job, Palace Keeper, it can get confusing and hard to determine what influences are right and which ones are wrong. We can get discouraged and even blinded by what is going on around us. When backed by God's Word, prayer, faith, repentance, baptism, the Holy Ghost, and obedience to the King, the tool of discernment can get easier to use because of the wisdom God has brought to us using those other tools. It will become clear which emotions are healthy and which ones are unhealthy for your heart. This leads us to the other tool God has for us, Palace Keeper. Do you feel more prepared for the job yet?

Chapter 21: Tools of a Palace Keeper-
Fellowship

**"Blessed is the man that walketh not in
the counsel of the ungodly, nor standeth in
the way of sinners, nor sitteth in the seat of
the scornful. But his delight is in the law of
the LORD; and in his law doth he meditate
day and night. And he shall be like a tree
planted by the rivers of water, that bringeth
forth his fruit in his season; his leaf also
shall not wither; and whatsoever he doeth
shall prosper" (Psalm 1:1-3).**

Relationships can be tough to discern. Many
times we don't see the hearts of the people we
associate ourselves with until it is much too late.
This is why discerning our emotions can be
very tricky. Sometimes we may not even be
that affected by those people who have
different standards and beliefs than ours. To
have proper fellowship may or may not be
about church people and non-church people. It
is about having those around you who take
care of their own hearts and are doing their job
as their own Palace Keepers so that together,
you both can glorify the Lord with your
relationship. Who we spend our time with is
very important to the condition of our hearts.
Being careful about where we go and how we
conduct ourselves is one thing, but also who we
are conducting ourselves with is crucial.

Okay, Palace Keeper, you are on the job. Let's just say that you are watching the front gate, on guard. You are focused and eager to please the King because you just finished having a one-to-one talk with Him. You cannot believe how great He is. You are in awe of His mercy and love for you. You are soaring inside!

Suddenly, you hear a rustling. An old friend of yours pops up right in front of the gate and peers through. Her face meets with yours, and the only thing between the two of you are the iron bars. She motions you closer, and you take a step forward. Her conversations are persuasive, and you find yourself starting to rethink your position. She reminds you of the good times you used to have together and how you have changed. She misses you and wants you to go with her. You tell her that you can't since you have a job to do, but that only makes her plead harder. Your hands tremble as you reach for the gate doors. *Do you open it for her?*

"Be ye not unequally yoked together with unbelievers: for what fellowship hath righteousness with unrighteousness? and what communion hath light with darkness?" (II Corinthians 6:14).

When God got a hold on my life and I started coming into the church, it was a very difficult decision for me to change who my friends were. The Lord showed me that this is not the case for everyone, but in my case, keeping some friends from my past could mean less growth for my spiritual future.

My old friends were very sweet and nice, but their involvement with the party scene would make it difficult for me to discern myself.

The fact is, we need people around us who will encourage our walk with God and not discourage it. Even some friends in the church can be hard to have if their dedication to God is not solid enough and they cause others around them to fall short of their potential. None of us is perfect, and we shouldn't dismiss a friendship, even from an unbeliever, just because he or she isn't as "spiritual" as we are. However, if the relationship with that particular person or group hinders your job as a Palace Keeper of your heart and slowly moves you out of God's hands, it is time to rethink if it is worth keeping. Remember this: *a healthy heart depends on healthy relationships.*

"If we say that we have fellowship with him, and walk in darkness, we lie, and do not the truth: but if we walk in the light, as he is in the light, we have fellowship one with another, and the blood of Jesus Christ his Son cleanseth us from all sin" (I John 1:6-7).

I have a story about a lady who I had met in the most unusual way. I became quite sick and ended up in the hospital. In those couple of days, I had my Bible by my side, yet after a while, I felt not just physically disconnected but also spiritually disconnected.

During my stay, I had to switch to a different floor. It was about 11:30 at night when I heard a knock at my door. A wonderful lady entered. She was a physician's assistant in the hospital and needed to take my vitals. She had just taken my temperature when she turned and spotted my Bible sitting on the table. This started a deep conversation about the Word of the Lord and about our testimonies.

She confessed to me that she was a good Christian for about five years, when all of a sudden she met a guy. They had been dating now for a long time, and he was not a believer. Also, they were not living the way she knew Jesus would approve of.

As I lay there in an unhealthy physical state, I realized that this encounter was confirmation of a burden the Lord had put in my heart a while earlier. It was a burden that had started this entire book project about the purity of our hearts, but I had put that burden on hold. Instead of this physician's assistant comforting me, seeing as I was the one sick physically, I found myself comforting and ministering to her spiritually.

I told her that the Lord would be with her through the trials but that having someone in God's place and having God second is unhealthy. I explained how Jesus grabbed a hold on my life and how I allowed Him inside to work and to change my heart.

For about an hour, this beautiful lady poured her heart out, crying about her current condition and how she felt. I could have easily told her that *I* was the one sick and she needed to be concerned with how *I* was feeling, but that is not what Jesus would have done. So by His graceful Spirit, I listened.

Sometimes, all we need is someone to listen to us. It is easy to depend on another person because he or she is there physically, in the flesh. We see the individual and hear that one right in front of us. We feel he or she can relate. Healthy relationships can provide loving ears. However, though it is important for us to fellowship and comfort each other, we should never fully depend on another person for our whole emotional fulfillment. Jesus is always there and wants to be our best friend. He will listen way better than any BFF!

To keep our emotions pure and clean, we have to be careful with being alone with others of the opposite sex and be careful about our conversations. I can remember liking a guy so much that I would just talk and pour my heart out to him during our phone calls. I would tell him secrets and give him so much personal information that my heart became an open door.
Looking back, I don't even think he told me half as much about himself. When we lost connection, I felt used and hurt. *Was that his fault or mine?* It was my own fault because I should have been on guard and wasn't. We should be careful how much information we reveal about ourselves and allow that data to flow at a steady pace. If that person is someone who respects you and is healthy for you, he shouldn't mind waiting to get to know you better.

Proper fellowship works with friends and those of the same sex as well. As people, we tend to feed off each other's emotions. *Have you ever been in a room with chatty, angry women who were in an uproar about what their husbands or boyfriends did?* After a while, that anger began to boil inside of you, and you didn't even know why! You may not even be in a relationship, but the environment is filled with a certain type of emotion so you feel it as well. Having proper fellowship will create an environment that is right, lighthearted, clean, and pure. Even better fellowship will invite the Lord's presence to partake. Ask yourself these questions about the people you currently fellowship with:

1.) Do they make me a better Christian?
2.) Do they love God by their actions and not just words?
3.) Do I find myself in compromising situations when I am with them?
4.) Am I always confused emotionally around them?
5.) Do I find myself thinking about them more than I think about God?

I encourage you to pray about these questions. Ask Jesus to reveal to your heart what to do. If you truly find yourself in an emotionally impure danger zone with someone or with your group, let them go! Your emotional health and your relationship with Jesus needs to come first. If they want to associate themselves with you, they have to respect your standards of living. Discernment will help us to choose those people to fellowship with. As a Palace Keeper, when we use discernment and yield to God's instruction, we can make the decision to surround ourselves with positive influences, hence proper fellowship. As we are doing our job, we will become more aware of who will help us do our job better or who distract us from doing our job altogether.

Okay, Palace Keeper, all of these tools we have discussed build up to the last one. If you exercise all the past tools properly in your heart, they will be able to build up godly standards to live by and stand upon.

Chapter 22: Tools of a Palace Keeper-
Standards

**"The statutes of the LORD are right,
rejoicing the heart: the commandment of the
LORD is pure, enlightening the eyes"
(Psalm 19:8).**

**"Blessed are they that keep his
testimonies, and that seek him with the
whole heart. They also do no iniquity: they
walk in his ways. Thou hast commanded us
to keep thy precepts diligently. O that my
ways were directed to keep thy statutes!"
(Psalm 119:2-5).**

**"Wherefore I was grieved with that
generation, and said, They do alway err in
their heart; and they have not known my
ways" (Hebrews 3:10).**

Rules, rules, rules! When I think of the word
"standards," I think of rules, which usually
means no fun for me. The more I walk with the
Lord, though, the more I understand that
standards represent something much deeper
than just rules. Standards are guidelines to how
you live, how you make your decisions, and the
level of respect you have for yourself and for
others.

We started this list of Palace Keeper tools that the King has provided with God's Word. Through God's Word, we learned that prayer was an important tool as well, which led into our faith. With faith in God's Word and prayer, we could then go to the Lord in repentance.

We can then clearly see that we need to be washed in baptism and receive the Holy Ghost. Obedience to the Scripture makes us more discerning when it comes to good and bad choices. Having discernment prepares the way for proper fellowship. We have come to this last tool of being a Palace Keeper, and it is what the rest of the tools create. This tool is **standards**.

Like I said before, when I think of standards I immediately think of rules. Here are some definitions of the word "standard" that may help us dig deeper:

1.) something considered by an authority or by general consent as a basis of comparison; an approved model

2.) standards, those morals, ethics, habits, etc., established by authority, custom, or an individual as acceptable

3.) something that stands or is placed upright

Standards are like beams that make up a building or a structure. Without beams, there will be no support between the foundation, the walls, and the roof. Remember, we cannot even start to build a structure without the foundation. A foundation is something solid that the beams can adhere to, like a concrete slab or flooring, a way of stabilization. The foundation for your standards can be found in the first tool of God's Word.

You have read who He is, and I hope by now you know what He expects from you. When we exercise all the tools on the list in our daily walk of emotional purity and in our spiritual walk with God, they will shape the standards we live by. You can say that keeping God's standards means *"walking the walk"*!

As a Palace Keeper, after using all the Palace Keeper tools, you will understand how high the bar is set for your emotional purity. You will begin to hold your head high when you are on the job because you have received the wisdom and knowledge needed to get the job done. Holding to the Lord's standards for purity increases your strength in standing every day for what you believe in.

"According as he hath chosen us in him before the foundation of the world, that we should be holy and without blame before him in love" (Ephesians 1:4).

Standards are how we live our lives. It's about our lifestyle and how we conduct ourselves. Palace Keeper, this has to be more than just a job that you go to every day, clock in, do your duty, and then clock out. Emotional purity needs to be a lifestyle choice. Have you ever heard the phrase, "You need to *be* the job"? We need to *be* a Palace Keeper, not just do it. That title needs to speak of who we are, not just what is required of us!

Look at the word within "standard." *Do you see it? Do you see the word "stand"?* It is time to stand for what God truly believes in! Stand up to preserving the purity of your palace! Stand firm in the foundation, in the Scripture, in God's Word! Stand on that solid Rock of refuge and truth! Stand now, not tomorrow or next year, but today. This means standing up and saying *no* to compromising relationships; to stand up and say *yes* to purity of your entire being by Jesus' standards. Protect yourself and be diligent with your relationship with God. Read His Word and apply it. Be a participant in what God is doing and not just a spectator. Say *yes* to growth, wisdom, God's love, and truth, in Jesus' name!

This is a list of some of the standards that the Bible tells us to uphold. God's standards should apply to our physical self and our spiritual self, our inside person and our outside person:

- Holiness
- Modesty
- Righteousness
- Compassion
- Broken / Contrite heart
- Careful lips
- Protected mind
- Praying spirit
- Careful eyes

It is very important to pray and seek the Lord about the standards that He wants to set in your palace. There may be more standards that God has for you that are not on this list. You have been doing your job for a while now, Palace Keeper. Just like a job in the real world, when you've been doing it long enough, the guidelines to perform that job are second nature. You don't have to try hard to obey the rules, and you don't have to read the company manual every time you have a question. You have a confidence that has grown, and you even find people coming to you for advice about what to do.

When we have standards as a Palace Keeper and live them daily, we may see a change in how we present ourselves. We grow a confidence in the Lord and His ways. We are bold to speak the gospel and to share with others what God has done. We can protect our palace because we know what our job is. We may even be able to help others realize that they need to be Palace Keepers for their hearts and show them how to work on their emotional purity.

Standing at the front gates, you hold all the tools you need to defeat impurity from your palace. You understand that your palace belongs to King Jesus, and you understand what He has asked of you. When bad influences and emotions come and try to get through your gates, you are equipped and ready for battle! You are unstoppable because you serve a King who is unshakable!

"With men this is impossible; but with God all things are possible" (Matthew 19:26).
"For the LORD will not forsake his people for his great name's sake: because it hath pleased the LORD to make you his people" (I Samuel 12:22).

"Let your conversation be without covetousness; and be content with such things as ye have: for he hath said, I will never leave thee, nor forsake thee" (Hebrews 13:5).

"For ye see your calling, brethren, how that not many wise men after the flesh, not many mighty, not many noble, are called: but God hath chosen the foolish things of the world to confound the wise; and God hath chosen the weak things of the world to confound the things which are mighty" (I Corinthians 1:26-27).

"For though we walk in the flesh, we do not war after the flesh: (for the weapons of our warfare are not carnal, but mighty through God to the pulling down of strong holds;) casting down imaginations, and every high thing that exalteth itself against the knowledge of God, and bringing into captivity every thought to the obedience of Christ; and having in a readiness to revenge all disobedience, when your obedience is fulfilled" (II Corinthians 10:3-6).

Chapter 23: Counting Our Accountability

We cannot afford to have a lack of accountability when it comes to our commitment to the Lord. To be accountable is to be responsible for your words and actions and how they influence other people's lives. *Lack of accountability* is the exact opposite. Being accountable, you are selfless because you are caring about how your words and actions affect others. When you are not accountable, you stay selfish, justifying your unhealthy emotional ways. It shows other people that you don't want to take the time to acknowledge what is inside your heart, and that can damage your current and future relationships.

A close friend of mine in the church had asked me to be her accountability partner. An "**accountability partner**" is someone with whom you are close, who can steer you back in God's direction if he or she ever sees you get off track or unfocused. Having an accountability partner may not be for everyone. It is a good idea if you feel like you are the type of person who needs an extra shove in the right direction and maybe needs a spiritual cheerleader. I agreed and asked if she could be mine as well. Having a good, godly friend who helps you in your walk with the Lord is great.

Think of it this way: If you are trying to be the best Palace Keeper for your heart and your friend is also trying to be her best Palace Keeper, there is an opportunity to keep both palaces pure and focused on the King. Just remember that if you choose to have an accountability partner, you first have to work to be accountable for yourself. There is still work you must do. The Lord will provide the change within that is needed. There is no doubt in that. He has done it in many examples in the Bible, and He will do it again! So don't worry whether or not the Lord will meet you when you seek Him. Just seek Him, and He will meet you! Guarding your heart is your responsibility. It is your job. God gave you that job.

"Behold, I stand at the door, and knock: if any man hear my voice, and open the door, I will come in to him, and will sup with him, and he with me" (Revelation 3:20).

"Let us therefore follow after the things which make for peace, and things wherewith one may edify another. For meat destroy not the work of God. All things indeed are pure; but it is evil for that man who eateth with offence. It is good neither to eat flesh, nor to drink wine, nor any thing whereby thy brother stumbleth, or is offended, or is made weak" (Romans 14:19-21).

The choice in how we respond to the demands of our job is up to us. The choice in how we guard our hearts is up to us. God will give us opportunities to progress in the areas we are weak. When we have Him as our focus by reading His written Word and following His direction, we have nothing to fear. We don't have to look down at the waves crashing. If we do, that is not God's fault. He is standing over you at all times with His hand reaching out. He has given the opportunity, and it is part of our job to recognize it and take it:

"Be strong and of a good courage, fear not, nor be afraid of them: for the LORD thy God, he it is that doth go with thee; he will not fail thee, nor forsake thee" (Deuteronomy 31:6).

Think about these questions. Seriously and honestly ask them to yourself. Try to be accountable for the answers:

1.) Do you find yourself thinking obsessively over someone other than God?

2.) Would you rather speak with a friend first than to God?

3.) When you first meet someone, do you tell him or her a lot about yourself?

4.) Are you constantly feeling like no one cares about you?

5.) When you're alone, do you feel uneasy and depressed?

6.) Even when you're in a crowd, do you feel alone?

7.) When you interact with people in conversations, do you find you do most of the talking?

Part of saying *"yes"* to these questions has to do with your state of mentality and how healthy it is. Now is time to have accountability for your actions and acknowledge that you are emotionally unhealthy.Emotions are more powerful than some people realize. It is what drives us across the country to visit sick family. It is what causes us to be heartbroken and weeping for hours through the night. The Lord has given our emotions much power and influence. Why? If they have the capacity to change someone's life so dramatically, why would the Lord allow emotions to exist so strongly?

In Proverbs 2, the Lord gives instructions and promises concerning wisdom. With the right wisdom, we can use our emotions the right way.

"My son, if thou wilt receive my words, and hide my commandment with thee; so that thou incline thine ear unto wisdom, and apply thine heart to understanding; yea, if thou criest after knowledge, and liftest up thy voice for understanding; if thou seekest her as silver, and searchest for her as for hid treasures; then shalt thou understand the fear of the LORD, and find the knowledge of God" (Proverbs 2:1-5).

When speaking about accountability, it can be a very daunting task. It requires us to step up to a responsibility that we all too often feel is too big for us. I pray that we can better prioritize what we need to focus on to get the job done right. The main thing about having accountability is having the knowledge of who is allowing you to be accountable. Having knowledge of who Jesus Christ really is will help us be accountable for our own actions, as Christ demonstrated through His own actions. Seeing how the Lord conducted Himself in His trials and tribulations will help us to see what we need to do in our own lives to take action.

"That your faith should not stand in the wisdom of men, but in the power of God" (I Corinthians 2:5).

"There is one body, and one Spirit, even as ye are called in one hope of your calling; one Lord, one faith, one baptism, one God and Father of all, who is above all, and through all, and in you all" (Ephesians 4:4-6).

"In the beginning was the Word, and the Word was with God, and the Word was God" (John 1:1).

"And the Word was made flesh, and dwelt among us, (and we beheld his glory, the glory as of the only begotten of the Father, full of grace and truth)" (John 1:14).

"For unto us a child is born, unto us a son is given: and the government shall be upon his shoulder: and his name shall be called Wonderful, Counseller, The mighty God, The everlasting Father, The Prince of Peace" (Isaiah 9:6).

"Ye are my witnesses, saith the LORD, and my servant whom I have chosen: that ye may know and believe ne, and understand that I am he: before me there was no God formed, neither shall there be after me. I, even I, am the LORD; and beside me is no saviour. I have declared, and have saved, and I have shewed, when there was no strange god among you: therefore ye are my witnesses, saith the LORD, that I am God" (Isaiah 43:10-12).

Being accountable for what you say and do is a big job. It requires you to be guided and trained in order to complete it well. We only walk this earth once and cannot possibly know everything beforehand. To be accountable for your heart and what goes in and out is exactly the same job that a palace guard has! Take responsibility for what you say and do.

Chapter 24: The Daily Commitment

"Delight thyself also in the LORD; and he shall give thee the desires of thine heart" (Psalm 37:4).

"For where your treasure is, there will your heart be also" (Matthew 6:21).

Obeying the Lord should be something that we do regardless of what the Lord will give us in return. Staying true to a commitment is a daily battle, one that requires much patience. As time goes on, the battle feels less strenuous and we are more in tune with the Lord. The commitment to stay emotionally and physically pure will be hard at first, but the more we keep going, the better things will get.

Here are some things that I learned to do to keep my focus on Jesus each day and my heart committed to Him first. Now remember, *diligence is the key*! No one is perfect except for Christ. Remember when Adam and Eve failed in the garden and ate the forbidden fruit? When they noticed that they were exposed, God clothed them. He can do the same for you!

"Unto Adam also and to his wife did the LORD God make coats of skins, and clothed them" (Genesis 3:21).

When reading the following list, it is important to have faith in the Lord Jesus and trust in Him. We can always go to His throne of mercy, but we must not take advantage of it by not doing our part. God wants us to seek Him continually for correction and change, praising Him in every aspect of our human life, especially during the difficult times.

Like Adam, we cannot stop doing the job assigned to us because of things we feel. God has asked us to guard our heart. Looking at different techniques to accomplish that should be taken into account. The ideas on this list are what helped me, and I pray by sharing them with you the suggestions may help you, too. They are in no special order:

1.) Keep a prayer journal

It is good to keep in mind that God knows our thoughts and we really don't have to speak a single word for Him to understand any messages that we have for Him. He already knows our motivations and intentions. My journal connects with Jesus in a nonverbal way.

First though, humbling yourself to verbal prayer has power in itself. When you verbally speak to God, there is an invitation for His Spirit to enter the atmosphere. Writing my thoughts and prayers on paper has been a true and honest practice. The journal should only be between you and God. Write Him a letter, jot down poems, passages of Scripture, quotes, anything that reminds you of the Lord or is inspired by Him.

Not everything has to be positive. Vent to Him. Ask Jesus to help you in the areas where you are weak. Tell Him in detail why you feel the way you do. If you're writing all positive things but something negative is really bothering you deep inside, guess what? God can see it! Be honest with Him and be up front about how you feel and what you want to change. He understands where you are and has promised to meet you there in order to bring you through. Ask Jesus for guidance in your relationships and for the true definition of emotional purity. Explain to God your circumstances and how you feel toward the significant people around you.

"That the blessing of Abraham might come on the Gentiles through Jesus Christ; that we might receive the promise of the Spirit through faith" (Galatians 3:14).

"Now we, brethren, as Isaac was, are the children of promise" (Galatians 4:28).

2.) Spread Scripture

When I had my own apartment, I put paper on the walls of my bedroom, and it became a wall Scripture scrapbook. I kept a little table near it, filled with old magazines, picture cutouts, letter cutouts, tape, glue, and markers. When a portion of Scripture caught my heart, I would run over, grab a marker, and sprawl it across the paper wall. The next morning I would wake up, and my soul was glad when the Scripture was the first thing in my thoughts.

Post it in your car on a sticky note or on your desk at work or in your school locker. Meditate on it, study it, and memorize it. God's Word will root in your heart, and by His power, your desires will change for the better. Ask the Lord to let the Scripture minister to your heart *and* mind. Part of protecting your heart is also filtering the right stuff inside your mind. Scripture is the right stuff!

Find those verses that relate to your situations. If you're feeling worthless, find passages about value and worth in God's eyes. If you're struggling with the right choices when you're dealing with the opposite sex, you can find many verses to keep your mind on Christ and His decisions for your life. Being open to the Scriptures and having a willing heart pleases God to the utmost.

"Then opened he their understanding, that they might understand the scriptures" (Luke 24:45). "Search the scriptures; for in them ye think ye have eternal life: and they are they which testify of me" (John 5:39).

3.) Read God's Word.

This one sounds so simple, but it's the most important thing on this list. Once you have prayed for guidance and the Scriptures are displayed, don't stop there. Study the Bible, His written Word, daily. If you're having a dry spiritual spell, you're not alone!

I cannot even type how many times that happens to me. Yet I continually read the Bible even if I don't feel like it. *Why?* Well, it is not about me. It is about Jesus and what *He wants*. It is God's commandment that we must read the Bible and apply it to our daily lives. It is not our power but the power of the Almighty God that ministers to us and does the work. What we must do is obey. It is great to have those meaningful verses that grab our attention, yet the Bible is full of encouraging and uplifting lessons that will also help your heart as well.

"I am the door: by me if any man enter in, he shall be saved" (John 10:9).
"Thy word have I hid in mine heart, that I might not sin against thee" (Psalm 119:11).

I created this list to help you in your daily connection with the Lord. We are required to acknowledge Him in our lives for two reasons: because *He is God, and we are not.* Point blank. What He says goes; there should be no in-between or turning around. Keep moving forward through the dry spiritual desert. Jesus will recognize that your heart is thirsty and will soon pour out His everlasting water and overflow your cup of need.

"Be not deceived; God is not mocked: for whatsoever a man soweth, that shall he also reap" (Galatians 6:7).

"They shall not hunger nor thirst; neither shall the heat nor sun smite them: for he that hath mercy on them shall lead them, even by the springs of water shall he guide them" (Isaiah 49:10).

"Jesus answered and said unto her, Whosoever drinketh of this water shall thirst again: but whosoever drinketh of the water that I shall give him shall never thirst; but the water that I shall give him shall be in him a well of water springing up into everlasting life" (John 4:13-14).

Chapter 25: Purity Security 101

Wow, Palace Keeper, you have come so far and now we are reaching the end of this book. You have learned a lot (hopefully!) and now it is time to take everything and put it into action. *Are you ready?*

I chose to name this last chapter "Purity Security" not only because it rhymed, which I thought was cool and funny, but also because we need to take this knowledge and pass it along. When I think of security, I think of big burly men with "security" black t-shirts on, moving fans along at a concert or event. Being a security guard is just like a palace guard, and part of their job is moving people who are stagnant and unmoving.

I am not telling you to put on a black t-shirt, stand on your sidewalk, and start physically pushing people past your house! Though hilarious, that would not be right. What I mean is: open your mouth and speak up about what you've learned while reading this book. Encourage your friends and family to be their own Palace Keepers; maybe even start a Palace Keeper Bible study group. If you do, contact me, because I'd love to hear about it!

The security guards whom I have seen usually bark orders and have some sort of authority. Instead of barking orders, compassionately speak to their hearts about what God has shown you. Also realize that gaining new insights from Christ gives you a responsibility to share that knowledge with others.

The people around us are going through difficult trials. Pray for them and ask the Lord to show them how to keep their hearts pure. Also, ask God to guide you in the situation, to open a door, that you may be used as a witness to explain about their being a Palace Keeper for their own hearts. Here are some open doors where you can talk about emotional purity.

You can reach out if you know someone who:

- is in a relationship
- just got out of a relationship
- is about to start a relationship
- is surrounded by bad influences
- is depressed, angry and hurt
- is suicidal
- who continually uses people
- who always needs friends around them
- doesn't think he/she has self-worth
- has compromised for a relationship
- who needs God

Before you check off this list and start blowing up people's phones, you need to keep your own emotions in check. Seek Jesus in prayer. When you do speak to someone about this, obey His instructions at all times.

I can remember when the Lord first gave this message to me. I took it and ran! Jesus was left in the dust, probably spinning from my impulsive leap. Jesus will give us the clean path to run on, and He will gladly run right next to us.

If your heart was pricked by something you read, take time with God and let Him sort it out inside you. The worst thing is thinking that you are helping someone when in fact you are adding to their unclean palace.

Be a good Palace Keeper by practicing what you're preaching! First and foremost, always take care of your emotional purity first. Hopefully, others will see how great a Palace Keeper you are and will approach you to learn what it takes to become one.

You may smile, gather your tools, and invite them to meet King Jesus.

Reference Bibliography

Almighty God, *The Holy Bible*

Definition references. *Dictionary. Merriam-Webster. The Free Dictionary.* [Online.] http://dictionary.reference.com; http://www.merriam-webster.com; http://www.thefreedictionary.com/

Emotional Purity and Anxiety, Where Are You?. [Online.] http://www.revelife.com/715923836/emotional-purity-and-anxiety-where-are-you/

Family First Aid. *Teen Self-Esteem.* [Online.] http://www.familyfirstaid.org/teen-self-esteem.html

Lee, Jordan. *Emotional Purity; Includes excerpt from "Before You Meet Prince Charming" by Sarah Mally.* [Online.] http://homeschoolblogger.com/growingingodliness/323660/

Mail Online. *Ralph Lauren apologizes for digitally retouching slender model to make her head look bigger than her waist.* [Online.] http://www.dailymail.co.uk/news/article-1219046/Ralph-Lauren-digitally-retouches-slender-model-make-look-THINNER.html

Samantha, Simply. Friday Favorite's.
[Online.]
http://justsimplysamantha.blogspot.com/2011/
03/friday-favorites_25.html
    The National Association of Self-Esteem
(NASE). *What is Self-Esteem?*. [Online.]
http://www.self-esteem-nase.org/what.php

Topol EJ (ed). *Cleveland Clinic Heart Book*
(2000) New York: Hyperion. *Textbook of
Cardiovascular Medicine* (1998), Philadelphia:
Lippincott-Raven.

Twain, Amy. *The Definition of Self-Esteem*.
[Online.]
http://www.selfgrowth.com/articles/definition_
self_esteem_0.html

Peacock, Bonnie. *The Key to Answered
Prayer* Bible Study. [Online.]